[Barnes, A. S.]

BLACK WOMEN

INTERPERSONAL RELATIONSHIPS IN PROFILE

a sociological study of work, home and the community

Wyndham Hall Press, Inc.

B L A C K   W O M E N

Interpersonal Relationships in Profile

by

Annie S. Barnes

Library of Congress
Catalog Card Number
85-051989

ISBN 0-932269-72-9

TABLE OF CONTENTS

PREFACE

Black women are known to have a number of strengths in varied settings. They are often the focus of home life and make enormous contributions to the community and workplace. Hence, this work is about the interpersonal relations of Black women in these environments. This is an important topic, because interpersonal relations impact the quality of life in each environment. As a result, I am deeply grateful to the Tidewater respondents who made this study possible by generously revealing the nature of interpersonal relations in these environments. The findings were combined with scholarly research by anthropologists, economists, psychologists, and sociologists to present a comprehensive picture of interpersonal relations important to Black women.

My special appreciation is also expressed to Dr. Demitri B. Shimkin, Professor of Anthropology at the University of Illinois, Urbana, who critiqued two drafts of this manuscript, and to Dr. Shepherd Krech, III, one of Professor Shimkin's students and Chair of the Anthropology Program at George Mason University, who also critiqued one draft of this work. Their comments were not only encouraging, but they also resulted in the total revision of the manuscript and several re-runs of the statistical data. I also owe a debt of gratitude to Dr. Alton Thompson, statistician, demographer, and Research Program Specialist at the North Carolina Agricultural and Technical State University, Greensboro, North Carolina, Dr. Charles Palit, Statistican and Head of the Survey Sampling Department at the Wisconsin Research Laboratory, University of Wisconsin, Madison, to Dr. Harold Rose, Professor of Urban Affairs, at the University of Wisconsin, Milwaukee, and Dr. James Nolan, Director of the Behavioral Science Laboratory, Norfolk State University for encouragement and assistance with data analysis, and to Dr. Marcus Alexis, who was then the first Black United States Government Interstate Commerce Commissioner, for reading the first draft of this manuscript and giving invaluable feedback and encouragement. Along with this marvelous encouragement and technical and scholarly assistance, it was my good fortune to get Dennis Reed, an English teacher at Morehouse College, Atlanta, Georgia, and a poet, to willingly take on the job of copy editing this work that resulted in its total revision and subsequent corrections and additions. Indeed, I am deeply thankful to my friend, Dennis, for his patient and detailed attention to this work.

Annie S. Barnes

LIST OF TABLES

vi

Dedicated to my Husband, Daughter, and Mother

.

CHAPTER ONE

BACKGROUND AND METHODOLOGY

Introduction

Constance E. Obudho, a social psychologist, has noted that references to Black relationships are found "on only a few pages and under a limited range of topics, such as fertility, illegitimacy, female-headed households, divorce, separation, lower-class status and child training" (1983:3). Allen (1983:86) and Addison (1983:109) also noted that there is not enough empirical research into the interpersonal relations in Black marriages. The available studies focus on "marital adjustment and decision making" (Rutledge 1983:239). As a result, "Sociologists have in many cases failed to study the depth of interpersonal relationships between the groups of people they analyze. They have, instead, tended to study the surface areas -- those aspects which can be easily defined, codified, and discussed" (Rodgers-Rose 1980:253). For example, "We know a great deal about financial and sexual aspects of marriage, but we know much less about what attracts an individual to another, what people are looking for in intimate relationships, and what qualities make for viable dialectic relationships" (Rodgers-Rose 1980:253-54). Also, anthropologists have described behavior among Blacks, including family, kinship, unwedded life, economic conditions, and voluntary associations, with little attention to the quality of such behavior. Because of our limited knowledge of the dynamics of Black relations, Addison (1983:109) stated that "more research on the Black family, particularly relating to interaction within the family as well as to the relationships of Black families to the socio-economic political institutions, is a pressing need." It is thus evident that neither is there enough knowledge about interpersonal relations in Black marriages, and nor is there any recent empirical information about the interpersonal relationship between employers and Black women and the dynamics of relations among Black women.

The question that such paucity of knowledge raises is why has there

1

been only cursory attention given to the relationships of Black women. It may be a consequence of our understanding that they are women of strength (Otterbein 1966:vii; Frazier 1939:102-113; Hipler 1974:47; Moynihan 1967:30-31; Powdermaker 1962:204), and often groups considered strong are described mainly in terms of their strengths. Another possible reason for the paucity of this research is that it is a sensitive issue not easily researched, for it involves important matters, such as dyadic and group interaction and interpersonal bonding.

To help fill this gap, the data in this study provide several perspectives into the relationships of Black women. They focus on stress, operationalized here as problems in Black women's interpersonal relations with other women and men in the workplace, interpersonal relations with their spouses in the home, and interpersonal relations with other Black women in the community, subjects treated in depth in the next chapters. However, research into the stress in interpersonal relations of Blacks is not an entirely new subject. A number of scholars, as early as the mid 1930s and early 1940s, considered it a significant research issue. Their perspective of the interpersonal relations of Blacks relates to behavior between the races as well as within the race. Due to segregation, interpersonal relations were described in the context of the caste system in the South. It is seen that Black female interpersonal relations were intricately related to the behavior between the races as well as within the race.

Historical Perspective of Interpersonal Relations

To begin this analysis of Black interpersonal relations, the caste system is examined. We found that whites made up the upper caste system while Blacks comprised the lower caste (Davis and the Gardners 1941:4-5). In effect, the system gave the upper caste greater access to privileges, duties, obligations, and opportunities than it gave lower caste members, and marriage and social mobility were forbidden between castes (Davis and the Gardners 1941:9). It also meant that the members of the lower caste experienced inequality in the courts and in the workplace (Kardiner and Ovesey 1962:61), and it was the job of the lower class, in the lower caste, to perform cheap laborious work, yet their standard of living was low (Dollard 1937:102-107). Hence, it was a function of the caste system to provide economic gains for the upper caste, and arrange citizens in "a superior and inferior group and regulate the behavior of the members of each group (Dollard 1937:62). The upper caste considered subordination of Negroes justifiable, for its members believed that Blacks were not only inferior to whites, but that they were also childlike; yet

2

Blacks worked to enhance the economic standing of whites. Consequently, relations between the races were at best contradictory.

The relationship between whites and mixed bloods was another type of interpersonal behavior between the races. The members of the upper caste were antagonistic toward mixed bloods, for they gave proof that in spite of endogamy, intermixture of the castes was slowly eliminating the physical differences that allowed them to subordinate Negroes (Davis and the Gardners 1941:41). In Old City, for example, "miscegenation caused Negroes to be less subordinate than Blacks in some other parts of the South and get along well with whites" (Davis and the Gardners 1941:39).

This historical perspective of Black interpersonal relations is also seen in their relations with each other. Several of the problems in our race replicate the attitudes and behavior of whites toward us. For example, like whites who attributed superior qualities to Negroes of mixed blood (Davis and the Gardners 1941:41), frequently members of the lower caste remarked that whites expected dark skin Negroes to act unsocialized more often than light skin Negroes (Davis and the Gardners 1941:21). And similarly, Black males began to prefer light skin women (Dollard 1937:140), which contributed immensely to divisiveness among Blacks, especially among our women.

The findings in the literature of the thirties and forties are also informative about interpersonal relations among Black women. The lower caste was comprised of a number of cliques ranked by prestige of members (Davis and the Gardners 1941:210). Their interpersonal relations were especially vivid in the behavior between female cliques; for example, the most prestigious female cliques and women immediately "below" them showed mutual antagonism. The conflict between the upper cliques and other women was also expressed by nonparticipation, contemptuous remarks, and subordination of the groups (Davis and the Gardners 1941:210). Besides interpersonal relations between cliques, the earlier literature also describes relations in female cliques. It was found that one feature of small clubs and cliques was that they were "Torn asunder by the mutual antagonism, rivalries, and the quest for leadership and prestige" (Kardiner and Ovesey 1962:64). In terms of group dynamics, this finding indicates that there was more stress in than between the cliques.

This historical perspective of Blacks also describes some of the interpersonal relations in the home, including husband and wife relationships. According to Doilard (1937:145,184), the practice that required Negro

3

men to be submissive, even though they were angry, because whites had taken their women, may have caused a wife to compare her husband with her potential ideal, a white lover, and Black men to compete with white men for the most attractive or better educated or better dressed Negro girls (Davis and the Gardners 1941:38). These findings suggest that stress characterized Black marriages early in this century, and that interpersonal relations between white men and Black women may have influenced Black marriage relationships.

Modern Perspectives of Interpersonal Relations

Unlike the thirties and forties, recent studies have not focused on interpersonal relations between the races and between female cliques. Instead, the empirical knowledge about the relations of Black women deals almost exclusively with interpersonal relations in Black marriages. Nevertheless, these studies were conducted around the time that this research was done and, therefore, together with the historical perspective, provide background information for this study.

There are two perspectives into Black marriage relationships in the contemporary literature. One view indicates effective interpersonal relations in Black marriages. Because they are important to the quality of life, Ruth King, a family therapist, and Jean Griffin (1983:11), a psychologist, noted that "Troubled relationships within Black romantic couples tend to extend into the marriage, the family, and beyond into employment spheres, educational settings, and social groups." Realizing the importance of a loving relationship for Black marriages, King and Griffin (1983:14) conducted a workshop as an intervention to improve Black loving relationships and a survey "to determine what Black people think and feel about love and loving relationships in the Black community" (1983:14). It was concluded that there are strong and healthy interactions in our marriages that "can off set negative forces that erode Black loving relationships" (King and Griffin 1983:20). According to Rutledge (1983:44,51), in a study conducted between 1968-69 in Detroit, Michigan, with 252 husbands and 256 wives, most of the "respondents experienced some level of happiness, with the husbands experiencing somewhat more happiness than the wives". Addison has also found loving relationships in Black marriages in Crescent City, Iowa. The Black men "were over-whelmingly described as not lazy, physically abusive, or big gamblers, as faithful and emotionally strong; however, the men were sometimes jealous and quick tempered" (Addison 1983:109).

Similarly, Turner and Turner (1983:35) found in a sample of Black

4

students at a large state university in the northeast in 1983, that "these young Black women are highly positive toward the expressive characteristics of men." In all Black marriages, spouses desire companionship, physical affection, and empathy from marriage (Scanzoni 1971:201). It seems clear that Black unmarrieds and marrieds desire warmth and affection in their relationships. Although some unmarried college women appear to derive these results from relationships with Black men, the research indicates some reservation in the minds of the respondents about the loving relations they experience in marriage. Nevertheless, the view in this literature is that Black marriages are loving relationships.

The second perspective presented in studies of Black marriages focuses on the dynamics of Black marriage relations. It suggests that couples, especially the wives, are experiencing some difficulty, but Black women are not negative about all the traits of Black men. For example, according to Turner and Turner (1983:35), in their study of Black coeds and white coeds, Black women had negative perceptions only about the "instrumental traits relevant to adequacy in the provider role." A counterbalancing view was found in Golden Towers, A Black middle class neighborhood in Atlanta. According to Barnes (1983:72), in the late 60s and in 1970, "the husbands in this neighborhood were good providers and cooperated in the performance of household chores; besides, they shared activities in and away from home." However, Barnes (1983:72) also noted that only a few couples experienced a strong emotional bond, attributed to the need for one spouse to assume major responsibility for managing the household. It also resulted from placing emphasis on material holdings, inequality in socioeconomic achievement, and lack of mutual friends. There is support in a number of other studies for marital dissatisfaction. According to Hippler (1974:42,49), because females denigrated male sexuality, and the men acted sullenly indifferent toward the women or resorted to bragging, it was impossible in Hunter's Point, a San Francisco housing project, to obtain deep emotional relations. Similarly, Bernard (1966:98) reported that wives suffer "deprivation in all areas, but is is relatively less marked in the area of companionship and love than in those of income and understanding." The achievement of a strong marital bond has been described as difficult because Blacks on the same social level as whites receive fewer dollars and less job satisfaction (Scanzoni 1971:305-309), and money, extramarital sex, and family problems result in the dissolution of some Black marriages (Holloman and Lewis 1978:223). However, it has been found that when the occupational, educational, and income status increases, marital cohesiveness does not improve in a corresponding manner

(Scanzoni 1971:201). Allen has also given evidence in his study of conjugal interpersonal relations from a sample of Chicago, Illinois, middle class Blacks and whites in 1974, in the middle years of the family cycle, that Black marriages are experiencing stress. For example, Allen (1983:86) concluded that "The incidence of second or successive marriages, children from prior unions, premature entry into marriages, and reported marital dissatisfaction all were higher for blacks."

Malveaux (1971:48,49) seems to sum up this counterbalancing view in the literature about interpersonal relations between us and our men. She found that some college women think they are exploited by Black men. It results from childhood socialization that teaches males and females to play games with each other, however, according to Malveaux, "this is the way that Black people relate to each other in all walks of life." What about the past? Malveaux (1971:48) stated that "circumstances forced Blacks to fake closeness which intensify unsurfaced animosity; now our feelings have surfaced and we are at each other's throats." The findings in this chapter, especially the data about stress in Black relations, indicate that we should focus on the elimination of the influence of white-Black relations on the attitudes of Blacks toward one another. It also appears that if we attribute all the stress in our relations with each other to the attitudes of whites toward us, we are likely to perpetuate the very behavior that we intend to eliminate. With this possibility, it may be useful to see whether we are creating problems among ourselves that are stress related.

This chapter has shown that the research of the sixties, seventies, and eighties represents two trends in our marriages. One trend addresses the loving relationships in our marriages while the second trend replicates the difficulty found in our earlier marriages. Though there are two trends, there is a larger literature on the second than on the first trend. In sum, the literature of the mid-thirties and early forties supports the trend between the late sixties and early eighties that stress characterizes relations between husbands and wives. More importantly, the literature of the Black family has begun to discuss the interpersonal relations in Black marriages. This is a step forward in obtaining more knowledge about our family that will enable us to do more for ourselves as we continue the struggle to overcome sex and racial barriers in our society.

Data Bases

The major data sources cited throughout this work were an interview study of interpersonal relations among Black women in Tidewater and a follow up interview study. Following a preliminary study (summer 1978, 80 respondents), I revised the interview schedule and, during the fall of 1978, my adult evening Family class helped administer it to 240 additional Black women in Tidewater, Virginia (Norfolk, Virginia Beach, Chesapeake, Portsmouth, Suffolk, and Hampton). The interviewers and go-betweens (members of the communities who helped obtain respondents) knew each participant in this study, a factor that likely enhanced its accuracy. According to the interviewers, acquaintanceship made it difficult for the respondents to misrepresent their behavior to people who knew them. We have support for this method. In the study of two small towns and Kansas City, for example, Martin and Martin (1978:2-3) selected families they had known for a long time. Similar to our rationale, they stated, "We believe our work was facilitated by our personal association with them, since they often gave us information that they might not have been willing to share with a stranger." Another dimension of this methodology is that instead of asking the respondents their specific answer to some questions, we asked them how they thought other Black women felt about the issues. The narrative in this study makes a distinction between the views of the respondents and the opinions they believe exist among Black women in Tidewater. The justification for using this approach to some questions was twofold: we felt that some respondents may be reluctant to answer extremely personal questions, and we assumed that they would describe the behavior of men and women with whom they had social affiliation. Besides, in almost all cases, when the respondents talked about other women, it was clear that such explanation described their own experiences and opinions, an assumption vividly supported in the data. The method of selecting the sample was also dictated to some extent by the length (23 single spaced pages, 146 questions, and 434 variables) of the interview schedule. We thus interviewed women whom we knew were willing to respond to such lengthy inquiry. When they made comments about questions, they or the interviewers sometimes wrote their responses on the back of their answer sheets. Upon completion of the interview process, between the fall of 1978 and the spring of 1981, twenty-seven follow-up interviews were conducted with the respondents. However, ten of the twenty seven women were not among the 240 participants in this study.* (§ see end of chapter for note.)

The socioeconomic characteristics of this sample are summarized in Table 1. Because it is difficult to get Blacks to give personal data, instead of asking the respondents their exact age, education, occupation, and income, we asked them to identify their personal data by categories. As noted in Table 1, by age, the sample ranges from twenty to over seventy years, but some 47.1 percent were between thirty and forty nine years of age. However, due to small cell figures, the age categories are collapsed; hence, in the next chapters, age will be described in terms of the respondents under and over forty years. Their schooling also indicates a wide range of educational achievement; therefore, the educational level of the respondents ranged from less than high school to college and graduate school. Similarly, the sample differs by type of employment and amount of earnings; hence, the respondents ranged from administrators to the unemployed, who earned $3,999 or less to over $19,000 annually.

Table 1

Socioeconomic Characteristics of Sample

Variable		Sample		Census		Sampling
		No.	%	No.	%	Error
Age	Under 40	162	68.1	* 46582	51.0	.002
	Over 40	76	31.9	* 44811	49.0	
Education	Less Than High School	42	17.6	** 1858	27.2	.005
	High School Graduate – Some College College Graduate– Graduate School	197	82.4	** 4975	72.8	
Occupation	Administration	20	8.6			
	Professional	66	28.3			
	White Collar	58	24.9			
	Blue Collar	15	6.4			
	Housewife	22	9.4			
	Unemployed	23	9.9			
	Other	29	12.4			
Income	Housewife	60	26.3			
	$3999 and Less	28	12.3			
	$4000 – $6999	31	13.6			
	$7000 – $9999	51	22.4			
	$10,000 – $12,999	24	10.5			
	$13,000 – $15,999	19	8.3			
	$16,000 – $18,999	6	2.6			
	$19,000 and over	9	3.9			

* U.S. Bureau of the Census, 1980 CENSUS OF POPULATION, "Characteristics of the Population, General Population Characteristics-Virginia, pp. 218, 220-224.
** U.S. Bureau of the Census, STATISTICAL ABSTRACT OF THE UNITED STATES, NATIONAL DATA BOOK AND GUIDE TO SOURCES, 100th Edition, 1979, p. 149.

This research also draws on my discussions with students in my Family course at Norfolk State University for more than a dozen years. This was an invaluable source of information, for they brought to the classroom the Tidewater point of view. In such sessions, we often debated the ideas that eventually comprised the interview schedule and discussed the findings that, according to the students, support their views of the interpersonal relations of Black women in Tidewater.

---

* We also used external data to determine the degree to which our respondents are representative of the remainder of the Tidewater Black female population. Because of the age distribution in the sample, the age intervals were collapsed to under forty and over forty; similarly, the education intervals were collapsed to less than high school to high school, some college education, a college degree, and graduate training. As a result, the accuracy (standard error) for the age and education variables were .002 and .005, respectively; occupation and income data by race and sex were not available. On the basis of the age and education variables, it appears that our sample is representative of black females in the Tidewater cities.

REFERENCES CITED

Allen, Walter R.

1983   "Race Differences in Husband-Wife Interpersonal Relationships During the Middle Years of Marriage." In Constance E. Obudho (ed.) BLACK MARRIAGE AND FAMILY THERAPY. Westport: Greenwood Press.

Addison, Donald P.

1983   "Black Wives: Perspectives About Their Husbands and Themselves." In Constance E. Obudho (ed.) BLACK MARRIAGE AND FAMILY THERAPY. Westport: Greenwood Press.

Barnes, Annie S.

1983   "Black Husbands and Wives: An Assessment of Marital Roles in A Middle Class Neighborhood." In Constance E. Obudho (ed.) BLACK MARRIAGE AND FAMILY THERAPY. Westport: Greenwood Press.

Bernard, Jessie

1966   MARRIAGE AND FAMILY AMONG NEGROES. Englewood Cliffs: Prentice-Hall.

Davis, Allison and Burleigh B. and Mary R. Gardner

1961   DEEP SOUTH. Chicago: The University of Chicago Press.

Dollard, John

1937   CASTE AND CLASS IN A SOUTHERN TOWN. New York: Doubleday and Company.

Frazier, E. Franklin

1939   THE NEGRO FAMILY IN THE UNITED STATES. Chicago: The University of Chicago Press.

Hippler, Arthur E.

1974   HUNTER'S POINT. New York: Basic Books, Inc.

Hollomon, Regina E. and Fannie E. Lewis

1978   "The Clan: Case Study of A Black Extended Family in
         Chicago." In Demitri B. Shimkin et al. (eds.) THE EX-
         TENDED FAMILY IN BLACK SOCIETIES. The Hague:
         Mouton Publishers.

Johnson, Charles S.

1941   GROWING UP IN THE BLACK BELT. New York: Schocken
         Books.

Kardiner, Abram and Lionel Ovesey

1962   THE MARK OF OPPRESSION. New York: The World
         Publishing Company.

King. Ruth E. G. and Jean T. Griffin

1983   "The Loving Relationship: Impetus for Black Marriage."
         In Constance E. Obudho (ed.) BLACK MARRIAGE AND
         FAMILY THERAPY. Westport: Greenwood Press.

Malveaux, Julianne

1973   "Polar Entities Apart", ESSENCE 4:48-49

Martin, Elmer P. and Joanne Mitchell Martin

1978   THE BLACK EXTENDED FAMILY. Chicago: The Univer-
         sity of Chicago Press.

Moynihan, Daniel Patrick

1967   "The Roots of the Problem." In Lee Rainwater and William
         L. Yancey (eds.) THE MOYNIHAN REPORT AND THE
         POLITICS OF CONTROVERSY. Cambridge: The M.I.T.
         Press.

Obudho, Constance E.

1983   BLACK MARRIAGE AND FAMILY THERAPY. Westport:
         Greenwood Press.

Otterbein, Keith F.

1966   THE ANDROS ISLANDERS. Lawrence: University of Kansas Publishers.

Powdermaker, Hortense

1966   COPPERTOWN: CHANGING AFRICA. New York: Harper & Row Publishers.

Rutledge, Essie Manuel

1983   "Husband and Wife Relationships of Black Men and Women." In Constance E. Obudho (ed.) BLACK MARRIAGE AND FAMILY THERAPY. Westport: Greenwood Press.

Scanzoni, John H.

1971   THE BLACK FAMILY IN MODERN SOCIETY. Boston: Allyn and Bacon.

Turner, Castellano B. and Barbara F. Turner

1983   "Black Families, Social Evaluations and Future Marital Relationships." In Constance E. Obudho (ed.) BLACK MARRIAGE AND FAMILY THERAPY. Westport: Greenwood Press.

CHAPTER TWO

BLACK WOMEN IN THE WORKPLACE

Introduction

From the mid 1930s to the early 1940s, Blacks experienced stress in both the larger society and the Black subsociety considered in Chapter 1. For married couples between the late sixties up to now, also discussed in Chapter 1, there are counterbalancing views about their interpersonal relations. One view is that Black marriages are healthy while another view holds that they are experiencing some difficulty. What can be concluded from these findings is that attention has been given to interpersonal relations between the races and between Black marriage partners. It can also be concluded that stress is an element in both sets of relationships. This chapter seeks to add a new dimension to the understanding of stress in interpersonal relations by focusing on behavior between Black women and their employers in the workplace. It contains an analysis of the literature of the Black experience in the workplace as well as an analysis of preferred employer types, interpersonal relations between employers and employees, job discrimination, job protest, and job satisfaction.

One of these issues has already been settled in the study of Blacks in the workplace -- they experience job discrimination. The empirical findings as well as the theoretical interpretations have focused on types of job discrimination. According to Marshall (1977:62), Blacks and whites are motivated to discriminate against Blacks on the basis of status, job, and other factors. One perspective into who discriminates against Blacks and other minorities focuses on hiring officials. It has been found that they use varied techniques of employment discrimination. According to Walker (1973:24), hiring officials discriminate against Blacks by utilizing test results to place job applicants in the unqualified category. Further, they use "aptitude or intelligence tests, without proving their relationship to predicting successful job performance" (Feagin and Feagin 1978:58), to hire and assign jobs.

This helps explain why a majority of "Black women have found their way into clerical and service jobs" (Beal 1957:7). Because Black women earn less than all employees (Chisholm 1970:41), it appears that job discrimination exploits them as an abundant, cheap source of labor (Hood 1978:46).

Another way that hiring officials keep Blacks from getting jobs is by hiring whites and paying them higher wages (Becker 1957:3,6). This practice causes Blacks to bear the greatest burden of unemployment and experience the heaviest deprivation in every sector of the economy (Hill 1977:18). Thus, a majority of Black women are either unemployed or work in low paying jobs.

Why do employers discriminate? One answer to this inquiry is that employers discriminate because they prefer "to be associated with some persons instead of others" (Becker 1957:3,6). On the other hand, Krueger (1963:483) has observed that, instead of distaste for contact with Blacks, discrimination "could be directed at maximizing white real income." For example, as Gibson (1978:20,22) has noted; "While white income comes primarily from employment in the managerial, administrative, professional, and technical classification, Black income comes primarily from the service workers classification." The assignment of whites to higher positions leads to higher income than is earned from jobs held by Blacks in service areas. Similarly, it has been postulated that discrimination results from envy-malice of employers against employees (Alexis 1974:81). In this case, to avoid some aspects of discrimination, minority workers can emphasize employer respect without compromising their integrity and obtain better jobs, promotions, and raises.

Another perspective into who discriminates against Blacks in the workplace concerns white employees. It argues that they can discriminate against Blacks by requiring government licensing or certification that favors them and works against Blacks. As a result, they can participate in workplace discrimination by also forcing employers to discriminate in hiring practices (Alexis 1974:73-74). Perhaps this type of job discrimination causes Blacks in urban areas to earn less income and experience even greater deprivations as the concentration of Blacks increases (Williams et al. 1974:68).

A related perspective into discrimination against Blacks in the workplace indicates that customers also discriminate against them by "paying higher prices to buy from whites" (Alexis 1974:81). When this occurs, employers earn enough to pay higher wages to employ whites and yet make a profit, which results in an increase in the unemployment rate among Blacks.

It has also been found that education is an element in workplace discrimination. Welch (1967:239) has pointed out that employers discriminate on the basis of the amount of education earned rather than in the quality of education obtained. For example, "lack of a high school diploma, college degree, graduate degree, or similar educational "union card" has been a barrier to employment" (Feagin and Feagin 1978:55). Although this is the case, there is some evidence that we can obtain a high level of education and yet experience discrimination in the workplace. For example, based on 1960 census data, Reed (1970:22-28) noted that Black female teachers had more education than white female teachers, "but lost out income wise, relative to white female teachers." Welch (1973:43) also argues that there is more discrimination in education than in the workplace. This observation is supported by Nunez (1974:16), who has noted that "few educators, Black and white alike, believe that the Black ghetto student can learn to write English as well as they can." He (1974:16) also stated that they "insure the fulfillment of this prophecy by convincing these students, that as a people, their strength lies in oral communication."

These divergent findings seem to indicate that discrimination in the workplace is a major problem facing Blacks in the American society. They also suggest that employers, employees, customers, and educational institutions discriminate against us and that its consequences affect not only our jobs, but also our earnings. Besides, these findings indicate that divergent ways are employed to discriminate against us in the workplace and comprise a system that assures our inequality.

The current research also provides a picture of job satisfaction among Black workers. It is conceptualized as intrinsic factors, including responsibilities, praise, and advancement and extrinsic factors such as salary, working conditions, fairness of company policies and practices and the nature of supervisors (Wernimont 1964:49). Unlike the findings about the types and causes of job discrimination, the empirical findings about job satisfaction are contradictory. One perspective "Tends to question Black motivation to work and the job attitudes once employment has been obtained" (Smith 1953:257). Ashe (1972:500), Slocum and Strawser (1972:31), and Weaver (1974:71-72) observed that Blacks rank lower needs, including pay, praise, and respect above such higher order needs as duty and satisfaction.

15

On the other hand, Lefcourt and Ladwig (1965:377-380), Champagne and King (1967:429,434), Friedlander and Greenberg (1971:292), and Greenhaus and Gavin (1972:449,452,455) present an opposing view of job satisfaction in the workplace. They noted that there is virtually no difference in job motivation between the races and, if it occurs, Blacks are merely facing reality. For example, "while blacks adhere as strongly as whites to the Protestant ethic values that attribute success to hard work, talent, and perseverance, they believe less often that such virtues will pay off for them (Gurin 1977:30). It is also likely that motivation is related to career counseling in public schools; for example, Shirley Chisholm (1970:41) has noted that "The racist counselor advises them (young Blacks and Puerto Ricans) to prepare for service-oriented occupations; he does not even consider the possibility of their entering the professions." A case in point is Bill Gaines who, at age 15, dropped out of school because his white counselor told him that his ambition to become a bus driver, engineer on a railroad, or a hockey or golf player was not possible. The counselor explained to Gaines that neither of the jobs was for Blacks and that the games he played were not games that Blacks play (Murphy 1971:30,32). Thus, it appears that improved public school counseling and comparable encouragement and rewards in the workplace would enhance motivation and intrinsic and extrinsic satisfaction among Black workers, including Black women.

A related perspective on job satisfaction in the workplace is that Blacks should also help themselves. As Boggs (1972:58) pointed out in his argument about the improvement of life for Blacks in cities, Blacks should "be self-reliant and encourage self reliance in the community." Boggs (1972:58) also noted that we should be encouraged to think beyond "Survival," because "we have made tremendous strides forward in clarifying the contradictions of the society." Hence, while encouraging whites to break down the many facets of discrimination that they implement in the workplace and public schools, we can do a great deal for ourselves by working hard and taking pride in job excellence. Bill Gaines has demonstrated how thinking and working hard enable us to get beyond the level of "Survival." It is true that the advice of his counselor prevented Gaines from pursuing relatively lucrative jobs, but he did not let it prevent him from working his way from a $48 a week janitor job to a $13,500 a year managerial job in a housing project in Boston. His job pride and job satisfaction are evident in his remark: "I would have called anyone a crazy nut (in the late fifties) who said, "I'd ever make $13,500 a year." Gaines not only worked hard, but he also obtained the support of his employers to achieve job satisfaction (Murphy 1971:32-33). It thus appears that

16

success in the workplace is a consequence of employers and employees working together for excellence.

This analysis has shown that "Racial membership has been treated as a causal factor" (Lefton 1968:348,350) in the workplace. Hence, racial affiliation, employer insensitivity to Blacks, ineffective career counseling, and lack of job motivation influence achievement and satisfaction. Although factors that influence job satisfaction have been identified, the effect of job discrimination on it has not been studied. Similarly, there has been virtually no empirical research about employer and employee relations, job discrimination, and job protest and satisfaction experienced by Black women who work for white male, Black male, Black female, and white female employers.

This apparent void in the literature determined the focus of this chapter. An attempt is made here to analyze the relationship between employer preferences and employer-employee interpersonal relations, job discrimination, job protest, and job satisfaction to determine whether Black women experience problems in the workplace. Job satisfaction was measured by the results obtained from varied types of protest while failure to complain about discrimination as well as protest was used as an index of dissatisfaction in the workplace. These questions were placed in the context of employer type and age and occupation of respondents.

Employer Preferences

We turn now to an analysis of the interpersonal relations that the Tidewater respondents experienced in the workplace with their preferred employer types. These data have been crosstabulated and put in tabular form. We summarized the crosstabulations by using the chi square test of significance. The findings were judged significant if the alpha value ranged from .0 to .05. A footnote to this methodology is that when crosstabulations of two variables were not found significant, they were used to comprise a panel in a table with similar data.

We began this analysis of interpersonal relationships in the workplace with employer preferences. An attempt was made to determine whether the preferences were significantly related to age of respondents. The employer preferences of the Tidewater respondents are crosstabulated with their age in Table 1. The data indicate that Black female employees in the sample preferred different employer types. However, they also indicate that the preferred employer types for

TABLE 1

Employer Preference by Age of Respondents

P A N E L		Age of Respondents					
		Under 40		Over 40		Total	
		No	%	No	%	No	%
A	White Male	61	42.4	21	31.3	82	38.9
B	Black Male	50	34.7	21	31.3	71	33.6
C	Black Female	21	14.6	10	14.9	31	14.7
D	White Female	12	8.3	15	22.4	27	12.8
	Total	144	68.2	67	31.8	211	100.0

Panel D: White Female
Corrected Chi Square =7.39258 with 1 degree of freedom
$P<0.0065$

Table Value:
Corrected Chi Square = 8.64567 with 3 degrees of freedom
$P<0.0344$

women under and over forty were not statistically significant, Panel D (White Female Employers) excepted (.01). Yet, they are informative for they tell us something about Black women's employer preferences. As also noted in Table 1, for example, because the largest percentage of women in both age categories preferred male to female employers, sex of employers was a distinguishing factor. On the other hand, race was only a slightly distinguishing factor, for 51 percent of the Tidewater respondents under forty and 54 percent over forty preferred white employers and 49 percent under forty and 46 percent over forty preferred Black employers. An attempt was made to further examine the findings in Table 1 by computing the corrected chi square and alpha value for all its data. The alpha value indicates that the collective findings on employer preferences by age of the respondents are

18

statistically significant (.03), and, therefore, we concluded that race, sex, and age are significantly related to employer choice.

Employer-Employee Interpersonal Relations

The respondents were asked why they prefer each employer type. They revealed that the nature of the interpersonal relationships between them and their preferred employer determined their choice. Interpersonal relations were operationalized in the interviews as compatibility (easy to get along with), equality, friendliness, and thanks and compliments for work. We were thus concerned with nonverbal as well as verbal interaction that trigger meaning in one person by another (Blubaugh and Pennington 1976:11). Maier (1965:15) has noted that "A leader (employer) interacts with an individual when he gives him instructions, makes an assignment, conducts an interview" and meets him informally in elevators and elsewhere. Maier (1965:15) has also indicated that a man's potential and the state of mind triggered in these interpersonal relations determine job performance. Because of this reason, this chapter considers at length the work relations between the Tidewater respondents and their preferred employer type.

When we crosstabulated the varied interpersonal relationships with employer types, none explicates that the relationships were statistically significant (see Table 2). However, the frequency distributions of the data are informative, for there is some variation by employer type. For example, the data in Table 2 indicate that white male employers were more compatible with the Tidewater respondents than other employer types. Fifty eight percent of the respondents who preferred working for them had found that they were easier to get along with than other employer types. A respondent in her twenties explained why she prefers working for white male employers:

I like white male employers because when they assign jobs, they are positive and stay with the original request; and they do not interfere with the personal business of their employees.

A public school teacher who is in her thirties also explained why she prefers white male employers:

I find that white male employers are easier to work with, because if something is said or done that is out of the way, you can quickly put them in their place, in a respectable way, and continue working for them.

19

Table 2

Interpersonal Relations Between Employers and Employees
By Employer Preference

P A N E L	Interpersonal Relations	Employer Preference							
		White Male		Black Male		Black Female		White Female	
		No	%	No	%	No	%	No	%
A	Compatibility:								
	Easier to Get Along With	43	57.3	26	38.2	10	37.0	9	34.6
	Not Eaiser to Get Along With	32	42.7	42	61.8	17	63.0	17	65.4
	Total	75	100.0	68	100.0	27	100.0	26	100.0
B	Equality:								
	Treated Employees as Equals	17	23.0	20	29.4	11	40.7	11	42.3
	Did Not Treat Employees as Equals	57	77.0	48	70.6	16	59.3	15	57.7
	Total	74	100.0	68	100.0	27	100.0	26	100.0
C	Friendliness:								
	Showed More Friendliness	18	24.3	19	27.9	7	25.9	4	15.4
	Did Not Show More Friendliness	56	75.7	49	72.1	20	74.1	22	84.6
	Total	74	100.0	68	100.0	27	100.0	26	100.0
D	Appreciation:								
	Gave More Thanks For Tasks Performed	34	45.9	26	38.2	8	29.6	13	50.0
	Did Not Give More Thanks For Tasks Performed	40	54.1	42	61.8	19	70.4	13	50.0
	Total	74	100.0	68	100.0	27	100.0	26	100.0
E	Compliments:								
	Gave More Compliments For Work	31	41.9	25	36.8	7	25.9	10	38.5
	Did Not Give More Compliments For Work	43	58.1	43	63.2	20	74.1	16	61.5
	Total	74	100.0	68	100.0	27	100.0	26	100.0

It appears that both respondents are arguing for compatible relations with their employers. Their work, the sample suggests, was easier and more enjoyable when employer-employee relations were compatible. Thirty eight percent of the respondents who prefer working for Black male employers and 37 percent who prefer Black female employers had found them easier to get along with than other employer types while 35 percent of the respondents who prefer working for white female employers considered them the most compatible type of employer (see Table 2).

We next determined whether the employers easiest to get along with are concentrated in particular occupations. These data are presented in Tables 3-6. This comparison of interpersonal relations between the Tidewater respondents and their employers show variation, indicated by employer type as well as by occupation of respondents. Only the responses from respondents who identified their specific occupation and answered the questions are reported in Tables 3-6. The remainder of the responses are reported in the Other category in the table, and its findings parallel the findings in the remainder of the table and, therefore, justify the small cell frequencies.

The data in Table 3 make it possible to determine how the women who prefer white male employers vary in interpersonal relations, including compatibility. They show that the respondents in administration (71 percent), social work (67 percent), teaching (56 percent), and domestic and clerical work (each 50 percent) had found them easier to get along with than the women in nursing (20 percent). As a result, a larger percentage of the respondents on the managerial level than in other occupations experienced compatibility with white male employers.

Compatibility is also a quality of interpersonal relations between Black male employers and the respondents who prefer them as employers. Looking at Table 4, we see that the respondents differ in the frequency that compatibility is expressed. It illustrates that the women in teaching (46 percent) and administration (43 percent) had found Black male employers easier to get along with than those in clerical work (23 percent) and nursing (20 percent). This analysis also indicates that two occupational groups, teachers and administrators, experienced about the same compatibility with their Black male employers.

The Black female employers were also compatible with the Tidewater respondents. Along with the Black male employers, they were the second most compatible employer type, but there were, of course, differences in compatibility in Table 5. Hence, the respondents in domestic work (100 percent) and clerical work (50 percent) had found Black female employers more compatible than the respondents in social work (33 percent) and teaching (20 percent). Unlike the respondents who prefer male employers, the respondents in service type jobs had found Black female employers easier to get along with than respondents at a higher level in the occupational structure.

Table 3
Interpersonal Relations Between White Male Employers
and Black Female Employees by Occupation

Interpersonal Qualities Panels	Admini- stration		Teaching		Social Work		Nursing		Clerical Work		Domestic Service		Other	
	No	%	No	%	No	%	No	%	No	%	No	%	No	%
A. Compatibility:														
Easier to Get Along With	5	71.4	5	55.6	2	66.7	1	20.0	8	50.0	2	50.0	19	63.3
Was Not Easier to Get Along With	2	28.6	4	44.4	1	33.3	4	80.0	8	50.0	2	50.0	11	36.7
Total	7	100.0	9	100.0	3	100.0	5	100.0	16	100.0	4	100.0	30	100.0
B. Equality:														
Treated Employ- ees as Equals	4	57.1	2	22.2	1	33.3	1	20.0	3	18.8	0	0.0	6	20.7
Did Not Treat Employees as Equals	3	42.9	7	77.8	2	66.7	4	80.0	13	81.2	4	100.0	23	79.3
Total	7	100.0	9	100.0	3	100.0	5	100.0	16	100.0	4	100.0	29	100.0
C. Friendliness:														
Showed More Friendliness	3	42.9	1	11.1	1	33.3	1	20.0	0	0.0	0	0.0	11	37.9
Did Not Show More Friendli- ness	4	57.1	8	88.9	2	66.7	4	80.0	16	100.0	4	100.0	18	62.1
Total	7	100.0	9	100.0	3	100.0	5	100.0	16	100.0	4	100.0	29	100.0
D. Appreciation:														
Gave More Thanks for Tasks Performed	3	42.9	4	44.4	1	33.3	3	60.0	8	50.0	2	50.0	12	41.4
Did Not Give More Thanks for Tasks Performed	4	57.1	5	55.6	2	66.7	2	40.0	8	50.0	2	50.0	17	58.6
Total	7	100.0	9	100.0	3	100.0	5	100.0	16	100.0	4	100.0	29	100.0
E. Compliments:														
Gave More Compliments for Work	3	42.9	3	33.3	2	66.7	4	80.0	5	31.2	2	50.0	11	37.9
Did Not Give More Compliments for Work	4	57.1	6	66.7	1	33.3	1	20.0	11	68.8	2	50.0	18	62.1
Total	7	100.0	9	100.0	3	100.0	5	100.0	16	100.0	4	100.0	29	100.0

Panel C: Corrected Chi Square = 22.03777 with 1 degree of freedom
$P < 0.0025$
Gamma = 0.32071

Table 4
Interpersonal Relations Between Black Male Employers and Black Female Employees by Occupation

Interpersonal Qualities Panels	Occupations: Administration No	%	Teaching No	%	Social Work No	%	Nursing No	%	Clerical Work No	%	Domestic Service No	%	Other No	%
A. Compatibility:														
Easier to Get Along With	3	42.9	6	46.2	0	0.0	1	20.0	3	23.1	0	0.0	11	44.0
Was Not Easier to Get Along With	4	57.1	7	53.8	2	100.0	4	80.0	10	76.9	2	100.0	14	56.0
Total	7	100.0	13	100.0	2	100.0	5	100.0	13	100.0	2	100.0	25	100.0
B. Equality:														
Treated Employees as Equals	3	42.9	4	30.8	0	0.0	2	40.0	3	23.1	0	0.0	7	28.0
Did Not Treat Employees as Equals	4	57.1	9	69.2	2	100.0	3	60.0	10	76.9	2	100.0	18	72.0
Total	7	100.0	13	100.0	2	100.0	5	100.0	13	100.0	2	100.0	25	100.0
C. Friendliness:														
Showed More Friendliness	3	42.9	4	30.8	0	0.0	2	40.0	4	30.8	0	0.0	5	20.0
Did Not Show More Friendliness	4	57.1	9	69.2	2	100.0	3	60.0	9	69.2	2	100.0	20	80.0
Total	7	100.0	13	100.0	2	100.0	5	100.0	13	100.0	2	100.0	25	100.0
D. Appreciation:														
Gave More Thanks for Tasks Performed	2	28.6	7	53.8	1	50.0	2	40.0	3	23.1	0	0.0	9	36.0
Did Not Give More Thanks for Tasks Performed	5	71.4	6	46.2	1	50.0	3	60.0	10	76.9	2	100.0	16	64.0
Total	7	100.0	13	100.0	2	100.0	5	100.0	13	100.0	2	100.0	25	100.0
E. Compliments:														
Gave More Compliments for Work	1	14.3	6	46.2	1	50.0	1	20.0	4	30.8	0	0.0	10	40.0
Did Not Give More Compliments for Work	6	85.7	7	53.8	1	50.0	4	80.0	9	69.2	2	100.0	15	60.0
Total	7	100.0	13	100.0	2	100.0	5	100.0	13	100.0	2	100.0	25	100.0

Table 5
Interpersonal Relations Between Black Female Employers
and Black Female Employees by Occupation

Interpersonal Qualities Panels	Admini- stration		Teaching		Social Work		Nursing		Clerical Work		Domestic Service		Other	
	No	%	No	%	No	%	No	%	No	%	No	%	No	%
A. Compatibility:														
Easier to Get Along With	0	0.0	1	20.0	1	33.3	0	0.0	2	50.0	2	100.0	4	40.0
Was Not Easier to Get Along With	1	100.0	4	80.0	2	66.7	1	100.0	2	50.0	0	0.0	6	60.0
Total	1	100.0	5	100.0	3	100.0	1	100.0	4	100.0	2	100.0	10	100.0
B. Equality:														
Treated Employ- ees as Equals	0	0.0	3	60.0	1	33.3	0	0.0	1	25.0	0	0.0	5	50.0
Did Not Treat Employees as Equals	1	100.0	2	40.0	2	66.7	1	100.0	3	75.0	2	100.0	5	50.0
Total	1	100.0	5	100.0	3	100.0	1	100.0	4	100.0	2	100.0	10	100.0
C. Friendliness:														
Showed More Friendliness	0	0.0	1	20.0	2	66.7	0	0.0	3	75.0	0	0.0	1	10.0
Did Not Show More Friendli- ness	1	100.0	4	80.0	1	33.3	1	100.0	1	25.0	2	100.0	9	90.0
Total	1	100.0	5	100.0	3	100.0	1	100.0	4	100.0	2	100.0	10	100.0
D. Appreciation:														
Gave More Thanks for Tasks Performed	0	0.0	1	20.0	1	33.3	0	0.0	2	50.0	0	0.0	3	30.0
Did Not Give More Thanks for Tasks Performed	1	100.0	4	80.0	2	66.7	1	100.0	2	50.0	2	100.0	7	70.0
Total	1	100.0	5	100.0	3	100.0	1	100.0	4	100.0	2	100.0	10	100.0
E. Compliments:														
Gave More Compliments for Work	0	0.0	1	20.0	1	33.3	0	0.0	2	50.0	0	0.0	2	20.0
Did Not Give More Compliments for Work	1	100.0	4	80.0	2	66.7	1	100.0	2	50.0	2	100.0	8	80.0
Total	1	100.0	5	100.0	3	100.0	1	100.0	4	100.0	2	100.0	10	100.0

On the other hand, the respondents who prefer white female employers had found them easier to get along with than other employer types. Table 6 presents the distribution of responses on the compatibility variable by occupation of respondents. It indicates that the teachers (50 percent) and nurses (25 percent) found white females the most compatible type of employer.

This analysis of all employer types by occupation reveals that, in terms of frequency of compatibility with particular occupational groups, the white female employers were more like male employers than Black female employers. They were more compatible with em- ployees high in the occupational structure while Black female employers were more compatible with lower ranking Black female employees in the occupational structure.

24

Interpersonal Qualities Panels	Administration		Teaching		Social Work		Nursing		Clerical Work		Domestic Service		Other	
	No	%	No	%	No	%	No	%	No	%	No	%	No	%
A. Compatibility:														
Easier to Get Along With	0	0.0	1	50.0	0	0.0	1	25.0	0	0.0	0	0.0	7	70.0
Was Not Easier to Get Along With	2	100.0	1	50.0	1	100.0	3	75.0	3	100.0	4	100.0	3	30.0
Total	2	100.0	2	100.0	1	100.0	4	100.0	3	100.0	4	100.0	10	100.0
B. Equality:														
Treated Employees as Equals	1	50.0	2	100.0	1	100.0	0	0.0	1	50.0	3	60.0	3	30.0
Did Not Treat Employees as Equals	1	50.0	0	0.0	0	0.0	4	100.0	1	50.0	2	40.0	7	70.0
Total	2	100.0	2	100.0	1	100.0	4	100.0	2	100.0	5	100.0	10	100.0
C. Friendliness:														
Showed More Friendliness	0	0.0	1	50.0	0	0.0	0	0.0	0	0.0	1	20.0	2	20.0
Did Not Show More Friendliness	2	100.0	1	50.0	1	100.0	4	100.0	2	100.0	4	80.0	8	80.0
Total	2	100.0	2	100.0	1	100.0	4	100.0	2	100.0	5	100.0	10	100.0
D. Appreciation:														
Gave More Thanks for Tasks Performed	2	100.0	0	0.0	0	0.0	2	50.0	1	50.0	4	80.0	4	40.0
Did Not Give More Thanks for Tasks Performed	0	0.0	2	100.0	1	100.0	2	50.0	1	50.0	1	20.0	6	60.0
Total	2	100.0	2	100.0	1	100.0	4	100.0	2	100.0	5	100.0	10	100.0
E. Compliments:														
Gave More Compliments for Work	1	50.0	1	50.0	1	100.0	2	50.0	1	50.0	2	40.0	2	20.0
Did Not Give More Compliments for Work	1	50.0	1	50.0	0	0.0	2	50.0	1	50.0	3	60.0	8	80.0
Total	2	100.0	2	100.0	1	100.0	4	100.0	2	100.0	5	100.0	10	100.0

Equality was the next interpersonal quality that we studied. We found that to some degree all employer types manifested this quality. The data in Table 2 indicate that white female employers treated the respondents (42 percent) who prefer working for them more like equals than Black female (41 percent), Black male (29 percent) and white male (23 percent) employers. The data also indicate that white male employers treated them less like equals while white female employers treated the respondents more like equals than Black employers. However, in general, a larger percentage of Black (70 percent) than white (65 percent) employers treated the respondents like equals (see Table 2). For the respondents treated like equals by their white female employers, Table 7 does show differences by age category. Sixty seven percent of the respondents under forty years of age reported equality in their relations with white female employers while 21 percent of the respondents over forty years had experienced equality in their relations. It appears that the younger women had shared a relationship of equality with white female employers more frequently than older women.

25

Table 7

White Female Employers Treat Black Female Employees
as Equals by Age of Respondents

| Equality Between White | Age of Respondents | | | | | |
| Female Employers and | Under 40 | | Over 40 | | Total | |
Black Female Employeees	No	%	No	%	No	%
Agree	8	66.7	3	21.4	11	42.3
Disagree	4	33.3	11	78.6	15	57.7
Total	12	46.2	14	53.8	26	100.0

Similar to age, there was some variation in this interpersonal quality by occupation. The data presented in Table 6 indicate that the frequency of equality between white female employers and the respondents was quite high; however, particular patterns were evident, especially for service type occupations, operationalized as "contributions to the welfare of others." They suggest that the respondents in service type jobs, such as social work (100 percent) and domestic work (60 percent), and teaching (100 percent), especially, were treated like equals. It is noteworthy, since we share the same sex status, that we get along well together.

Similar to white female employers, a large percentage of Black female employers also treated their employees like equals. The data in Table 5 reinforce the findings in this study about the variation in interpersonal characteristics by occupation of respondents. They show that the respondents treated like equals and prefer Black female employers were teachers (60 percent), social workers (33 percent), and clerical workers (25 percent). Likewise, Table 4 illustrates the extent that respondents who prefer Black male employers varied in their treatment as equals. The administrators (43 percent), nurses (40 percent), teachers (31 percent), and clerical workers (23 percent) told us that Black male employers treated them like equals while respondents in other occupations did not note equality in their interpersonal relations. These data also indicate that the respondents in administration experienced this relationship more often than other respondents, but the relation is almost evenly known by the respondents in administration and nursing.

White male employers, though less often than other employers, also

26

treated their respondents as equals in the workplace. However, the respondents in administration (57 percent), social work (33 percent), teaching (22 percent), nursing (20 percent), and clerical work (19 percent) were more likely to be treated like equals by their white male employers than domestic workers (see Table 3).

This analysis of the equality characteristic of employers suggests that a relatively high status among the respondents in the occupational structure was usually associated with equality between them and their employers.

Friendliness is another interpersonal quality of employers in the Tidewater sample. We found that all employer types were friendly with their employees (see Table 2). Nevertheless, Black male employers were friendlier than all other employer types; 28 percent of the respondents who prefer working for them reported that they were the friendliest employers, however, the data presented in Table 4 show variation by occupation of respondents. A larger percentage of the administrators (43 percent) and nurses (40 percent) experienced friendliness with Black male employers than teachers and clerical workers (each 31 percent.)

Black female employers were the second friendliest employer type (26 percent). Of course, as indicated in Table 5, some respondents had found them friendlier than others; for example, a larger percentage of clerical workers (75 percent) and social workers (67 percent) had found them friendlier than teachers (20 percent).

On the other hand, 24 percent of the respondents who prefer white male employers had found them friendlier than other employers (see Table 2). Further, the data in Table 3 make it possible to compare the expression of friendliness by occupation of respondents. They show that a relatively large percentage of the respondents in administration (43 percent), social work (33 percent), nursing (20 percent), and teaching (11 percent) had found white male employers friendly while clerical and domestic workers did not note friendliness.

As would be expected, friendliness was also characteristic of interpersonal relations between the respondents in this Tidewater study and their white female employers (see Table 2). Fifteen percent of the respondents who prefer working for them stated that they were friendlier than other employers. There were, however, differences in the percentage of respondents by occupation who reported friendliness as a characteristic of their relationship with white female employ-

27

ers. Thus, as Table 6 indicates, 50 percent of the respondents in teaching and 20 percent of the respondents in domestic work found white female employers the friendliest employers. As noted in Table 2, this analysis also indicates that Black male and female employers were friendlier toward the respondents in the workplace than white employers.

On the other hand, the white female employers expressed more appreciation (thanks) than all other employer types. Of the respondents who prefer white female employers, 50 percent reported that they had expressed thanks for their work (see Table 2). The data in Table 6 indicate that although a relatively high percentage of the respondents in four occupational categories had received thanks more frequently than other employers for their work, the respondents in administration (100 percent) and domestic work (80 percent) experienced the greatest frequency.

We also found that white male employers (46 percent) show more appreciation for tasks accomplished in the workplace than Black employers. Likewise, Table 3 illustrates that there was some variation by occupation of the respondents. Those employed in nursing (60 percent) and in clerical and domestic work (each 50 percent) received appreciation more frequently for their work than other respondents. Nevertheless, compared to Black employers, a relatively large percentage of respondents in each occupation received thanks for their work from white male employers.

The Black male employers in Tidewater ranked third in the expression of appreciation for work. Thirty eight percent of the respondents who prefer them as employers noted that they expressed more thanks than all other employer types (see Table 2). There was some variation by occupation of respondents in Table 4. Hence, the respondents in teaching (54 percent), social work (50 percent), and nursing (40 percent) received more thanks than the respondents in administration (29 percent) and clerical work (23 percent) for their labor.

Appreciation was also characteristic of the relations between Black female employers and the Tidewater respondents. However, the frequency (30 percent) that the Black female employers thanked the respondents for their work was quite low (see Table 2). There were, of course, differences in the percentage of respondents who received thanks by occupation in Table 5. Among the respondents who prefer working for them, only clerical workers (50 percent), social workers (33 percent), and teachers (20 percent) noted that they expressed appreciation for their work. As shown in Table 2, 30 percent of the respondents agreed that Black female employers expressed thanks for their work compared to 50 percent of white female employers. In fact, white employers of both sexes expressed more thanks for the respondent's work than Black employers.

Compliments on the way tasks were performed was another type of interpersonal relationship between the Tidewater respondents and their employers. The data in Table 2 indicate that white male employers were more complimentary (42 percent) than white female (39 percent), Black male (37 percent) and Black female (26 percent) employers. The employer types also show variation by occupational affiliation of the respondents. As illustrated in Table 3, some respondents who prefer white male employers received more compliments for their work than other respondents. Thus, the respondents in nursing (80 percent), social work (67 percent), and domestic work (50 percent) were given compliments more frequently than the respondents in administration (43 percent), teaching (33 percent), and clerical work (31 percent). In summary, a relatively large percentage of the respondents in each occupational category received compliments on their work from white male employers.

Table 6 illustrates that white female employers also vary in the frequency they compliment the respondents. We found that 100 percent of the social workers and 50 percent each of the administrators, teachers, nurses and clerical workers, and 40 percent of the domestic workers received compliments on their work. Again, the complimentary relationship between white female employers and the respondents enhance behavior between us and our white female counterparts. The result is likely to impact productivity and the quality of life in the workplace.

The Black male employers of the Tidewater respondents also differed by occupations in giving them compliments on their work. As can be seen in Table 4, the respondents in social work (50 percent) and teaching (46 percent) received more compliments on job performance than the respondents in clerical work (31 percent), nursing (20 percent), and administration (14 percent).

Similar to all other employer types, there was variation by occupational affiliation in Black females' expression of compliments to the Tidewater respondents. For example, as noted in Table 5, clerical workers (50 percent), social workers (33 percent), and teachers (20 percent) were the only respondents who received compliments. Moreover, the respondents with the highest position in the occupational structure were complimented less frequently than other respondents.

Because Black female employers and Black female employees occupy the same race and sex status, we desired to find out more about their work relationship. Specifically, as shown in Tables 8-10, we determined the perspective that each group had of the other. According to 88 percent of the respondents under forty and 76 percent over forty, Black women in Tidewater would not do domestic work for other Black women (see Table 8). In support, the alpha value (.05) indicates a significant relationship between age and the opinion of the respondents on this variable. An implication of this finding is that older women were more likely to do domestic work for Black women than younger women. Nevertheless, a relatively large percentage of the women in both age groups did not perform domestic work for other Black women. The next problem that the respondents say that Black women had with Black female employees in Tidewater was that they did not work efficiently for them (see Table 8). Of this group, there was virtually no difference between the percentage of women under forty (70 percent) as compared with the women over forty (71 percent) with this view. There is still another problem, resentment, that Black female employers experienced with Black female employees. We found that there was more agreement among the respondents on this variable than on the preceding variables. Therefore, we found that 100 percent of the women in both age groups reported that Black female employees resented the superior standing of their Black female employers. For example, one respondent noted that "Black female employers let their jobs go to their head." Similarly, all the respondents who answered this question agreed that Black female employees were jealous of the achievement of their Black employers (see Table 8).

A counterbalancing view was also given by the respondents. They reported that Black female employers in Tidewater also caused problems for Black female employees. As shown in Table 9, some problems often developed, in the opinion of the respondents, because they spoke too harshly to their Black female employees. A woman, for example, in her twenties, who does clerical work, said:

> Black female employers treat Black subordinates harshly. This is seen when they embarass them in public for making mistakes, and they never treat us as adults.

Of the 86 respondents who answered this question, 100 percent of the women in both age groups agreed that the communication of Black female employers with their Black female employees was too harsh (see Table 9). As can also be seen in Table 9, the respondents (100 percent) reported that Black female employers in Tidewater

Table 8

The Respondents' Perception of Ways Black Female Employers
Perceive Black Female Employees by Age of Respondents

P A N E L	Perceptions	Age of Respondents					
		Under 40		Over 40		Total	
		No	%	No	%	No	%
A	Will Do Domestic Work for Black Women	15	11.9	16	24.2	31	16.1
	Will Not Do Domestic Work for Black Women	111	88.1	50	75.8	161	83.9
	Total	126	65.6	66	34.4	192	100.0
B	Work Efficiently for Black Women	42	30.4	18	29.0	60	30.0
	Do Not Work Efficiently for Black Women	96	69.6	44	71.0	140	70.0
	Total	138	69.0	62	31.0	200	100.0
C	Resent Superiority of Black Female Employers	57	100.0	27	100.0	84	100.0
	Do Not Resent Superiority of Black Female Employers	0	0.0	0	0.0	0	0.0
	Total	57	67.9	27	32.1	84	100.0
D	Show Jealousy of Black Female Employer's Achievement	65	100.0	24	100.0	89	100.0
	Do Not Show Jealousy of Black Female Employers' Achievement	0	0.0	0	0.0	0	0.0
	Total	65	73.0	24	27.0	89	100.0

Panel A: Corrected Chi Square = 4.00097 with 1 degree of freedom
         $P < 0.0455$

assigned too much work to Black female employees. Both findings add a new dimension to the earlier data about the interpersonal relations between Black female employers and employees. They suggest that Black female employees also experienced problems with Black female employers; hence, there is likely to be mutual antagonism in the workplace. If, indeed, this is the case, they experience unpleasant working conditions, which may account, in part, for their level of productivity, quality of work, and job satisfaction.

It may be useful to consider the impact of Black female employer-employee interpersonal relations on job success. We may find that

Table 9

Respondents' Perception of Ways Black Female Employees
Perceive Black Female Employers by Age of Respondents

P A N E L	Perceptions	Age of Respondents					
		Under 40		Over 40		Total	
		No.	%	No.	%	No.	%
A	Speak too Harshly	62	100.0	24	100.0	86	100.0
	Do Not Speak too Harshly	0	0.0	0	0.0	0	0.0
	Total	62	72.1	24	27.9	86	100.0
B	Require too Much Work	24	100.0	13	100.0	37	100.0
	Do Not Require too Much Work	0	0.0	0	0.0	0	0.0
	Total	24	64.9	13	25.1	37	100.0

white racism is compounded by another brand, but equally detrimental form of racism, Black female racism. According to Vontress (1971:12), "in-fighting among Blacks is simply self-rejection, a reflection of hatred which whites have for Blacks." Vontress (1971:12) has also noted that "As products of a racist society, we have acquired the same cultural attributes as have whites, including "anti-black sentiments." Not only has "in-fighting" among Blacks been identified, but some suggestions have been made to enhance interpersonal relations in the community and in the home. Wesley (1960:144) has suggested a campaign for decency for better manners and better conduct, among youth and adults, to improve interpersonal relations among Blacks in the community while Vontress (1971:16) has recommended "a massive program similar to that launched by Muslims" to help black men and women to respect their roles as fathers and mothers, and as husbands and wives." Besides, we can do a great deal for ourselves by enhancing mutual unity that would also improve interpersonal relations between Black employers and black employees.

These findings about Black employer-employee relations offer still another insight. They indicate that there are paradoxes in the workplace behavior of Black women. For example, as shown in Table 10, though Black female employees complained and resented the superior standing of Black female employers, they expected more consideration of work tardiness and absence from them than from white female employers. Of the women under 40, 36 percent expected

Table 10

A Comparsion of Employee Expectations from Black Female
Employers and White Female Employers by Age of
Respondents

P a n e l	Expectations	Age of Respondents					
		Under 40		Over 40		Total	
		No.	%	No	%	No	%
A	Expect More Consideration of Work Tardiness and Absence from Black Female Employers	48	36.4	11	23.9	59	33.1
	Do Not Expect More Consideration of Work Tardiness and Absence from Black Female Employers	84	63.6	35	76.1	119	66.9
	Total	132	74.2	46	25.8	178	100.0
B	Expect More Consideration of Work Tardiness and Absence from White Female Employers	21	16.2	7	13.0	28	15.2
	Do Not Expect More Consideration of Work Tardiness and Absence from White Female Employers	109	83.8	47	87.0	156	84.8
	Total	130	70.7	54	29.3	184	100.0

such favors from Black female employers while 16 percent expected
the same favors from white female employers. Similarly, of the
women over 40, 24 percent expected both types of favors from their
Black female employers, compared to 13 percent who expected the
same favors from their white female employers (see Table 10). Because
all of us need each other's help, it seems that it would be useful for
us to employ campaigns or similar techniques, as suggested by Vontress
and Wesley, to make it easier for us to obtain intra-racial support.
This may be an important step in the enhancement of sex, race, and
interracial relations.

Job Discrimination

The types of job discrimination as well as their occurrence in different
occupational settings afford another perspective of the interpersonal
relations of the Tidewater respondents. The position of the Black
female worker -- her effort to get jobs, her work assignment, her
work load, her work hours, and her wages, raises, and promotions
-- can best be understood in terms of the age of workers and occupa-

tional groups. The types of job discrimination that the respondents had experienced under all employer types are analyzed first and then separately by occupation, but only the currently employed are included in this analysis. Moreover, the same methodology is used to report crosstabulations for job discrimination as was employed to describe interpersonal relations.

The discrimination practices suggested in the theoretical discussion, at the beginning of this chapter, appear to be supported by these data. For example, as shown in Table 11, the respondents experienced varied types of work discrimination, with all employer types, including failure to get jobs. The failure to get jobs was operationalized in the interviews as the process of either making application or requesting a job and, due to being unqualified or because there were no openings, did not receive it. Although the respondents had failed to get jobs with all employers, there was some variation by employer type. Of the respondents who had failed to get a job, a larger percentage who prefer white female employers (16 percent) and white male and Black female employers (each 10 percent) had this experience than respondents who prefer Black male (4.4 percent) employers in Table 11. This finding also indicates that the likelihood of getting a job also varied by sex of employer, which means that failure to get a job occurred slightly more often when employers were females than when they were males. As noted in Table 12, among the respondents who prefer white female employers, those in administration (40 percent) and social work (17 percent) had failed to get jobs more often than respondents in nursing and clerical (each 11 percent) and domestic (9 percent) work. Similarly, as shown in Table 13, the respondents who prefer Black female employers also differed in the frequency they failed to get employment with them. It indicates that 22 percent of the administrators, 12 percent of the domestic workers, and 7 percent of the clerical workers noted that they had applied for jobs to work for Black female employers, but did not receive them. As shown in Table 14, the percentage of respondents who prefer white male employers and failed to get jobs was relatively low. Of this group, the social workers (11 percent) had this experience more often than other respondents. Further, as presented in Table 15, of the respondents who prefer Black male employers, only two groups, social workers (40 percent) and clerical workers (5 percent), had applied for and failed to get jobs with them. This analysis indicates some other findings about the experience of the Tidewater respondents in the workplace. As noted in Tables 12 and 13, a larger percentage of administrators than other employees failed to get jobs under both types of female employers while the male employers had usually

34

Table 11

Job Discrimination by Employer Preference

P A N E L	Types of Job Discrimination	White Male No.	%	Black Male No.	%	Black Female No.	%	White Female No.	%
A	Job:								
	Failed to Get a Job	15	9.5	5	4.4	10	10.1	17	15.9
	Did Not Fail to Get a Job	143	90.5	109	95.6	89	89.9	90	84.1
	Total	158	100.0	114	100.0	99	100.0	107	100.0
B	Higher Duties:								
	Failed to Get Assigned to Job with Higher Duties	31	19.6	18	15.8	19	19.2	26	24.3
	Did Not Fail to Get assigned to a Job with Higher Duties	127	80.4	96	84.2	80	80.8	81	75.7
	Total	158	100.0	114	100.0	99	100.0	107	100.0
C	Amount of Work:								
	Assigned an Unusual Amount of Work	75	47.5	50	43.9	38	38.4	41	38.3
	Was Not Assigned an Unusual Amount of Work	83	52.5	64	56.1	61	61.6	66	61.7
	Total	158	100.0	114	100.0	99	100.0	107	100.0
D	Working Hours:								
	Worked Long Hours	29	18.4	30	26.3	15	15.2	29	27.1
	Did Not Work Long Hours	129	81.6	84	73.7	84	84.8	78	72.9
	Total	158	100.0	114	100.0	99	100.0	107	100.0
E	Wages:								
	Received Low Wages	21	13.3	24	21.1	14	14.1	27	25.2
	Did Not Receive Low Wages	137	86.7	90	78.9	85	85.9	80	74.8
	Total	158	100.0	114	100.0	99	100.0	107	100.0
F	Raise:								
	Failed to Get a Raise	44	27.8	19	16.7	17	17.2	25	23.4
	Did Not Fail to Get a Raise	114	72.2	95	83.3	82	82.8	82	76.6
	Total	158	100.0	114	100.0	99	100.0	107	100.0
G	Raise on Time:								
	Failed to Get a Raise on Time	48	30.4	21	18.4	17	17.0	40	37.4
	Did Not Fail to Get a Raise on Time	110	69.6	93	81.6	83	83.0	67	62.6
	Total	158	100.0	114	100.0	100	100.0	107	100.0
H	Promotion:								
	Failed to Get a Promotion or Get it on Time	33	20.9	26	22.8	16	16.2	29	27.1
	Did Not Fail to Get a Promotion or Get it on Time	125	79.1	88	77.2	83	83.8	78	72.9
	Total	158	100.0	114	100.0	99	100.0	107	100.0

Panel B: White Male
    Corrected Chi Square = 4.58881 with 1 degree of freedom
      $P < 0.0322$
   White Female
    Corrected Chi Square = 4.52911 with 1 degree of freedom
      $P < 0.0333$
Panel F: White Female
    Corrected Chi Square = 5.43878 with 1 degree of freedom
      $P < 0.0197$
Panel G: White Female
    Corrected Chi Square = 5.67036 with 1 degree of freedom
      $P < 0.0173$

35

Table 12
Job Discrimination Experienced by Respondents Who Prefer
White Female Employers by Occupation

Job Discrimination Panels	Admini-stration No	%	Teaching No	%	Social Work No	%	Nursing No	%	Clerical Work No	%	Domestic Service No	%	Other No	%
A. Employment:														
Failed to Get a Job	4	40.0	1	6.3	1	16.7	1	11.1	1	11.1	1	9.1	8	17.4
Did Not Fail to Get a Job	6	60.0	15	93.7	5	83.3	8	88.9	8	88.9	10	90.9	38	82.6
Total	10	100.0	16	100.0	6	100.0	9	100.0	9	100.0	11	100.0	46	100.0
B. Duties Assigned:														
Was Not Assigned Jobs With Higher Duties	4	40.0	2	12.5	3	50.0	1	11.1	4	44.4	4	36.4	8	17.4
Assigned Jobs With Higher Duties	6	60.0	14	87.5	3	50.0	8	88.9	5	55.6	7	63.6	38	82.6
Total	10	100.0	16	100.0	6	100.0	9	100.0	9	100.0	11	100.0	46	100.0
C. Work Assigned:														
Assigned Too Much Work	5	50.0	5	31.2	5	83.3	5	55.6	3	33.3	4	36.4	14	30.4
Was Not Assigned Too Much Work	5	50.0	11	68.8	1	16.7	4	44.4	6	66.7	7	63.6	32	69.6
Total	10	100.0	16	100.0	6	100.0	9	100.0	9	100.0	11	100.0	46	100.0
D. Work Hours:														
Assigned Long Work Hours	5	50.0	3	18.8	3	50.0	2	22.2	0	0.0	3	27.3	12	26.1
Was Not Assigned Long Work Hours	5	50.0	13	81.2	3	50.0	7	77.8	9	100.0	8	72.7	34	73.9
Total	10	100.0	16	100.0	6	100.0	9	100.0	9	100.0	11	100.0	46	100.0
E. Pay:														
Paid Low Wages	6	60.0	1	6.3	3	50.0	1	11.1	0	0.0	4	36.4	11	23.9
Was Not Paid Low Wages	4	40.0	15	93.7	3	50.0	8	88.9	9	100.0	7	63.6	35	76.1
Total	10	100.0	16	100.0	6	100.0	9	100.0	9	100.0	11	100.0	46	100.0
F. Pay Increase:														
Failed to Get a Raise	2	20.0	1	6.3	2	33.3	0	0.0	0	0.0	5	45.5	14	30.4
Did Not Fail to Get a Raise	8	80.0	15	93.7	4	66.7	9	100.0	9	100.0	6	54.5	32	69.6
Total	10	100.0	16	100.0	6	100.0	9	100.0	9	100.0	11	100.0	46	100.0
G. Time of Pay Increase:														
Failed to Get a Raise on Time	3	30.0	3	18.8	3	50.0	3	33.3	2	22.2	7	63.6	18	39.1
Did Not Fail to Get a Raise on Time	7	70.0	13	81.2	3	50.0	6	66.7	7	77.8	4	36.4	28	60.9
Total	10	100.0	16	100.0	6	100.0	9	100.0	9	100.0	11	100.0	46	100.0
H. Promotions:														
Promotions Were Too Slow	4	40.0	4	25.0	4	66.7	2	22.2	2	22.2	3	27.3	9	19.6
Promotions Were Not Too Slow	6	60.0	12	75.0	2	33.3	7	77.8	7	77.8	8	72.7	37	80.4
Total	10	100.0	16	100.0	6	100.0	9	100.0	9	100.0	11	100.0	46	100.0

Panel E: Corrected Chi Square = 17.59475 with 7 degrees of freedom
P < 0.0139
Gamma = -0.04253

failed to give the respondents in social work jobs more often than respondents in other occupations. However, there was very little difference between the percentage of administrators (69 percent) and social workers (68 percent) denied employment by all employer types.

Denial of employment is not a new phenomenon in the American society. As early as the pre-World War II period, Blacks migrated to cities in search of jobs, but a majority failed to get employment. They were "around on the streets or sat on the stoops or under the trees in the park" while a few lucky ones received low paying jobs (Boggs 1972:55). Since that time, especially in the last 15 years, the employment picture has not changed very much. For example, automation and cybernation decreased the number of young Black males and females employed in Atlanta (Boggs 1972:55). Furthermore,

Table 13
Job Discrimination Experienced by Respondents Who Prefer
Black Female Employers by Occupation

Job Discrimination Panels	Administration		Teaching		Social Work		Nursing		Clerical Work		Domestic Service		Other	
	No	%	No	%	No	%	No	%	No	%	No	%	No	%
A. Employment:														
Failed to Get a Job	2	22.2	0	0.0	0	0.0	0	0.0	1	7.1	1	12.5	6	15.8
Did Not Fail to Get a Job	7	77.8	16	100.0	6	100.0	7	100.0	13	92.9	7	87.5	32	84.2
Total	9	100.0	16	100.0	6	100.0	7	100.0	14	100.0	8	100.0	38	100.0
B. Duties Assigned:														
Was Not Assigned Jobs With Higher Duties	5	55.6	1	6.3	3	50.0	1	14.3	0	0.0	1	12.5	8	21.1
Assigned Jobs With Higher Duties	4	44.4	15	93.7	3	50.0	6	85.7	14	100.0	7	87.5	30	78.9
Total	9	100.0	16	100.0	6	100.0	7	100.0	14	100.0	8	100.0	38	100.0
C. Work Assigned:														
Assigned Too Much Work	3	33.3	4	25.0	2	33.3	4	57.1	8	57.1	2	25.0	14	36.8
Was Not Assigned Too Much Work	6	66.7	12	75.0	4	66.7	3	42.9	6	42.9	6	75.0	24	63.2
Total	9	100.0	16	100.0	6	100.0	7	100.0	14	100.0	8	100.0	38	100.0
D. Work Hours:														
Assigned Long Work Hours	2	22.2	1	6.3	2	33.3	2	28.6	2	14.3	1	12.5	5	13.2
Was Not Assigned Long Work Hours	7	77.8	15	93.7	4	66.7	5	71.4	12	85.7	7	87.5	33	86.8
Total	9	100.0	16	100.0	6	100.0	7	100.0	14	100.0	8	100.0	38	100.0
E. Pay:														
Paid Low Wages	5	55.6	1	6.3	1	16.7	2	28.6	1	7.1	1	12.5	3	7.9
Was Not Paid Low Wages	4	44.4	15	93.7	5	83.3	5	71.4	13	92.9	7	87.5	35	92.1
Total	9	100.0	16	100.0	6	100.0	7	100.0	14	100.0	8	100.0	38	100.0
F. Pay Increase:														
Failed to Get a Raise	1	11.1	1	6.3	1	16.7	1	14.3	4	28.6	2	25.0	7	18.4
Did Not Fail to Get a Raise	8	88.9	15	93.7	5	83.3	6	85.7	10	71.4	6	75.0	31	81.6
Total	9	100.0	16	100.0	6	100.0	7	100.0	14	100.0	8	100.0	38	100.0
G. Time of Pay Increase:														
Failed to Get a Raise on Time	1	11.1	3	18.8	2	33.3	0	0.0	1	7.1	3	37.5	7	18.4
Did Not Fail to Get a Raise on Time	8	88.9	13	81.2	4	66.7	7	100.0	13	92.9	5	62.5	31	81.6
Total	9	100.0	16	100.0	6	100.0	7	100.0	14	100.0	8	100.0	38	100.0
H. Promotions:														
Promotions Were Too Slow	1	11.1	3	18.8	3	50.0	0	0.0	2	14.3	1	12.5	6	15.8
Promotions Were Not Too Slow	8	88.9	13	81.2	3	50.0	7	100.0	12	85.7	7	87.5	32	84.2
Total	9	100.0	16	100.0	6	100.0	7	100.0	14	100.0	8	100.0	38	100.0

Panel B: Corrected Chi Square = 17.98479 with 7 degrees of freedom
$P < 0.0120$
Gamma = -0.08939
Panel E: Corrected Chi Square = 16.48948 with 7 degrees of freedom
$P < 0.0210$
Gamma = -0.39296

"unemployment is more severe among black women than among black men or white women and nonwhite girls have the highest rate of unemployment" (Pressman 1970:104). Black women can also become unemployed because they are "clustered in the social service occupations as teachers, counselors, social workers and nurses which are easily phased out" (Nunez 1978:14). The occupations of the Tidewater respondents, as seen in Tables 12-15, support the observation that Black women are clustered in social service type occupations. This finding is also supported by the occupational structure in Atlanta. It indicates, for example, several differences between Black and white females (Atlanta Urban Employment Survey 1968-69:8). According to Barnes (1977:355), based on this survey, over 45 percent more white females than Black females held white collar positions. Further, white females

Table 14
Job Discrimination Experienced by Respondents Who Prefer
White Male Employers by Occupation

Job Discrimination Panels	Administration		Teaching		Social Work		Nursing		Clerical Work		Domestic Service		Other	
	No	%	No	%	No	%	No	%	No	%	No	%	No	%
A. Employment:														
Failed to Get a Job	1	7.1	1	4.8	1	11.1	1	6.7	2	8.3	0	0.0	8	13.1
Did Not Fail to Get a Job	13	92.9	20	95.2	8	88.9	14	93.3	22	91.7	10	100.0	53	86.9
Total	14	100.0	21	100.0	9	100.0	15	100.0	24	100.0	10	100.0	61	100.0
B. Duties Assigned:														
Was Not Assigned Jobs With Higher Duties	3	21.4	7	33.3	1	11.1	2	13.3	8	32.0	2	20.0	6	9.8
Assigned Jobs With Higher Duties	11	78.6	14	66.7	8	88.9	13	86.7	16	68.0	8	80.0	55	90.2
Total	14	100.0	21	100.0	9	100.0	15	100.0	24	100.0	10	100.0	61	100.0
C. Work Assigned:														
Assigned Too Much Work	9	64.3	7	33.3	4	44.4	12	80.0	9	37.5	4	40.0	27	44.3
Was Not Assigned Too Much Work	5	35.7	14	66.7	5	55.6	3	20.0	15	62.5	6	60.0	34	55.7
Total	14	100.0	21	100.0	9	100.0	15	100.0	24	100.0	10	100.0	61	100.0
D. Work Hours:														
Assigned Long Work Hours	3	21.4	3	14.3	1	11.1	4	26.7	3	12.5	1	10.0	13	21.3
Was Not Assigned Long Work Hours	11	78.6	18	85.7	8	88.9	11	73.3	21	87.5	9	90.0	48	78.7
Total	14	100.0	21	100.0	9	100.0	15	100.0	24	100.0	10	100.0	61	100.0
E. Pay:														
Paid Low Wages	2	14.3	0	0.0	2	22.2	2	13.3	3	12.5	1	10.0	10	16.4
Was Not Paid Low Wages	12	85.7	21	100.0	7	77.8	13	86.7	21	87.5	9	90.0	51	83.6
Total	14	100.0	21	100.0	9	100.0	15	100.0	24	100.0	10	100.0	61	100.0
F. Pay Increase:														
Failed to Get a Raise	3	21.4	4	19.0	4	44.4	4	26.7	3	12.5	6	60.0	17	27.9
Did Not Fail to Get a Raise	11	78.6	17	81.0	5	55.6	11	73.3	21	87.5	4	40.0	44	72.1
Total	14	100.0	21	100.0	9	100.0	15	100.0	24	100.0	10	100.0	61	100.0
G. Time of Pay Increase:														
Failed to Get a Raise on Time	2	14.3	1	4.8	6	66.7	6	40.0	5	20.8	2	20.0	24	39.3
Did Not Fail to Get a Raise on Time	12	85.7	20	95.2	3	33.3	9	60.0	19	79.2	8	80.0	37	60.7
Total	14	100.0	21	100.0	9	100.0	15	100.0	24	100.0	10	100.0	61	100.0
H. Promotions:														
Promotions Were Too Slow	3	21.4	1	4.8	4	44.4	3	20.0	6	25.0	1	10.0	13	21.3
Promotions Were Not Too Slow	11	78.6	20	95.2	5	55.6	12	80.0	18	75.0	9	90.0	48	78.7
Total	14	100.0	21	100.0	9	100.0	15	100.0	24	100.0	10	100.0	61	100.0

Panel G: Corrected Chi Square = 19.57640 with 7 degrees of freedom
P < 0.0038
Gamma = 0.28896

(5.7 percent) held approximately four times as many managerial and proprietal positions as Black females (1.5 percent). Barnes (1977:355) also noted that "more black females (17.7 percent) than white females (10.5 percent) held blue collar jobs;" and Black females (49.8 percent) also held more than four times as many service work jobs as white females (11.5 percent). Consequently, a larger percentage of white females than Black females held prestigious and/or authority-bearing positions." Billingsley (1968:88) attributed this pattern to "disparity in the quality of education offered Negroes and whites and discrimination in the occupational structure;" that is, "Negroes with similar education as whites do not have similar job opportunities."

As a result of unequal job opportunities, along with the large and growing number of "unemployed" and "unemployable" school "drop outs," transients, and recent arrivals in the ghetto, "a black lumpenpro-

Table 15

Table 15
Job Discrimination Experienced by Respondents Who Prefer
Black Male Employers by Occupation

Job Discrimination Panels	Admini- stration No	%	Teaching No	%	Social Work No	%	Nursing No	%	Clerical Work No	%	Domestic Service No	%	Other No	%
A. Employment:														
Failed to Get a Job	0	0.0	0	0.0	2	40.0	0	0.0	1	4.8	0	0.0	2	4.4
Did Not Fail to Get a Job	9	100.0	14	100.0	3	60.0	10	100.0	20	95.2	8	100.0	43	95.6
Total	9	100.0	14	100.0	5	100.0	10	100.0	21	100.0	8	100.0	45	100.0
B. Duties Assigned:														
Was Not Assigned Jobs With Higher Duties	1	11.1	1	7.1	2	40.0	1	10.0	6	28.6	1	12.5	6	13.3
Assigned Jobs With Higher Duties	8	88.9	13	92.9	3	60.0	9	90.0	15	71.4	7	87.5	39	86.7
Total	9	100.0	14	100.0	5	100.0	10	100.0	21	100.0	8	100.0	45	100.0
C. Work Assigned:														
Assigned Too Much Work	5	55.6	8	57.1	3	60.0	7	70.0	9	42.9	0	0.0	17	37.8
Was Not Assigned Too Much Work	4	44.4	6	42.9	2	40.0	3	30.0	12	57.1	8	100.0	28	62.2
Total	9	100.0	14	100.0	5	100.0	10	100.0	21	100.0	8	100.0	45	100.0
D. Work Hours:														
Assigned Long Work Hours	5	55.6	5	35.7	1	20.0	4	40.0	5	23.8	1	12.5	9	20.0
Was Not Assigned Long Work Hours	4	44.4	9	64.3	4	80.0	6	60.0	16	76.2	7	87.5	36	80.0
Total	9	100.0	14	100.0	5	100.0	10	100.0	21	100.0	8	100.0	45	100.0
E. Pay:														
Paid Low Wages	4	44.4	4	28.6	3	60.0	3	30.0	3	14.3	0	0.0	7	15.6
Was Not Paid Low Wages	5	55.6	10	71.4	2	40.0	7	70.0	18	85.7	8	100.0	38	84.4
Total	9	100.0	14	100.0	5	100.0	10	100.0	21	100.0	8	100.0	45	100.0
F. Pay Increase:														
Failed to Get a Raise	0	0.0	2	14.3	1	20.0	0	0.0	8	38.1	2	25.0	6	13.3
Did Not Fail to Get a Raise	9	100.0	12	85.7	4	80.0	10	100.0	13	61.9	6	75.0	39	86.7
Total	9	100.0	14	100.0	5	100.0	10	100.0	21	100.0	8	100.0	45	100.0
G. Time of Pay Increase:														
Failed to Get a Raise on Time	2	22.2	1	7.1	2	40.0	1	10.0	1	4.8	2	25.0	12	26.7
Did Not Fail to Get a Raise on Time	7	77.8	13	92.9	3	60.0	9	90.0	20	95.2	6	75.0	33	73.3
Total	9	100.0	14	100.0	5	100.0	10	100.0	21	100.0	8	100.0	45	100.0
H. Promotions:														
Promotions Were Too Slow	2	22.2	1	7.1	1	20.0	3	30.0	4	19.0	2	25.0	13	28.9
Promotions Were Not Too Slow	7	77.8	13	92.9	4	80.0	7	70.0	17	81.0	6	75.0	32	71.1
Total	9	100.0	14	100.0	5	100.0	10	100.0	21	100.0	8	100.0	45	100.0

Panel A: Corrected Chi Square = 20.97016 with 7 degrees of freedom
         P < 0.0066
         Gamma = -0.11579
Panel C: Corrected Chi Square = 15.48578 with 7 degrees of freedom
         P < 0.0303
         Gamma = -0.19322
Panel D: Corrected Chi Square = 14.06682 with 7 degrees of freedom
         P < 0.0500
         Gamma = -0.21016

letariat has also developed (Munford 1972:14). What is most difficult is that "Except for constant agitation for action and public recognition of this problem by the NAACP, and a few such other community organizations, there is little evidence of real concern in the larger community" (CRISIS 1961:114). These findings suggest that denial of employment or employment in jobs that are easy to phase out along with a growing class of poor people have not caused much concern in either the wider community or Black subsociety.

The Tidewater respondents also noted that they experienced problems on their jobs. Some of them were related directly to their work, such as job assignments, work load, and work hours. Concerning work assignments, the respondents were asked whether they were assigned jobs with higher duties than they were given at the beginning of their employment. Although their job description had allowed them to do other types of work, they often were not given much chance. There was, however, some variation by employer type in Table 11. Twenty four percent of the respondents who prefer white female employers, 20 percent who prefer white male employers, and 19 percent who prefer Black female employers had not been assigned jobs with higher duties while only 16 percent who prefer Black male employers noted the same experience. Hence, the white employers and Black female employers were more alike than employers by race; in fact, there was more similarity in this practice between white male and Black female employers than between opposite sex employers of the same race. When we crosstabulated age with the failure of employers to assign the respondents jobs with higher duties, only the data pertaining to white employers were statistically significant. As indicated in Tables 16 and 17, the alpha value (.03) shows a significant relationship between both employer types and the job assignment variable. As can also be seen in Tables 16 and 17, a larger percentage of the respondents who prefer white male and white female employers under forty than over forty stated that they had not been assigned jobs with higher duties. Moreover, the percentage of respondents who had not been given such assignments was almost three times higher among women under forty than over forty.

There was, however, some variation by occupation. As shown in Table 12, of the respondents who prefer white female employers, the highest percentage not assigned jobs with higher duties were employed in social work (50 percent), clerical work (44 percent), and administration (40 percent). Table 14 shows the occupational distribution of the respondents who prefer white male employers. The largest percentage not assigned jobs with higher duties were teachers and clerical workers (each 33 percent), and administrators (21 percent). Similar to white female employers, as Table 13 indicates, the largest percentage of the respondents who prefer Black female employers and not assigned jobs with higher duties were in administration (56 percent), social work (50 percent), and nursing (14 percent). On the other hand, it is seen in Table 15 that the largest percentage of the respondents with this experience and prefer Black male employers were social workers (40 percent), clerical workers (29 percent), and domestic workers (13 percent). This analysis also suggests that social workers comprised one group that most often failed to be assigned jobs with higher duties while administrators were another group that was not

Table 16

White Male Employers Do Not Assign Black Women to
Jobs With Higher Duties by Age of Respondents

Fewer Assignments With Higher Duties	Age of Respondents					
	Under 40		Over 40		Total	
	No.	%	No.	%	No.	%
Agree	27	24.5	4	8.3	31	19.6
Disagree	83	75.5	44	91.7	127	80.4
Total	110	69.6	48	30.4	158	100.0

Corrected Chi Square = 4.58881 with 1 degree of freedom
P < 0.0322

Table 17

White Female Employers Do Not Assign Black Women to
Jobs With Higher Duties by Age of Respondents

Failed to Assign Employees to Higher Duties	Age of Respondents					
	Under 40		Over 40		Total	
	No.	%	No.	%	No.	%
Agree	22	31.4	4	10.8	26	24.3
Disagree	48	68.6	33	89.2	81	75.7
Total	70	65.4	37	34.6	107	100.0

Corrected Chi Square = 4.52911 with 1 degree of freedom
P < 0.0333

41

assigned jobs with higher duties than the ones given at the time of employment.

Another problem that relates to the job itself is the work load. It was operationalized in the interviews as assignment of too much work. Forty eight percent of the respondents who prefer white male employers, 44 percent who prefer Black male employers, and 38 percent each of the respondents who prefer Black female and white female employers had been assigned too much work (see Table 11). Of course, this experience also varied by occupation of respondents; hence, as can be seen in Table 14, the largest percentage of the respondents who prefer white male employers and assigned too much work were in nursing (80 percent), administration (64 percent), and domestic work (44 percent). On the other hand, as documented in Table 15, the respondents who prefer Black male employers and assigned too much work were nurses (70 percent), social workers (60 percent), teachers (57 percent), administrators (56 percent), and clerical workers (43 percent). It is interesting to note that, as shown in Table 13, a larger percentage of all respondents who prefer Black female employers, including nurses and clerical workers (each 57 percent), had also been assigned too much work. As a result, the respondents in nursing had been assssigned too much work by Black male and Black female employers. Similarly, as indicated in Table 12, of the respondents who prefer white female employers, the largest percentage assigned too much work were in social work (83 percent), nursing (56 percent), and administration (50 percent). More frequently than not, the respondents in nursing and administration were recipients of too much work from both white employer types than respondents in the remainder of the occupations. Moreover, a larger percentage of both male employer types and Black female employers had assigned the respondents in nursing too much work.

Long work hours were another job related problem experienced by the Tidewater respondents. They were operationalized in the interview as requests to stay after work, without pay. Again, Table 11 presents findings that suggest variation by employer type on this variable. For example, the respondents who prefer white female employers (27 percent) and Black male employers (26 percent) were asked to work over time without pay more frequently than the respondents who prefer white male (18 percent) and Black female employers (15 percent). Likewise, regarding long work hours, we found variation by occupation. It is seen in Table 12 that, of the respondents who prefer white female employers and worked long hours, the highest percentage were in administration, social work (each 50 percent) and

42

domestic workers (27 percent); the largest percentage of respondents who prefer Black male employers and worked long hours were in administration (56 percent), nursing (40 percent), and teaching (36 percent) in Table 15. The major consequence is that a higher percentage of the respondents in administration and social work were assigned long work hours by white female employers and Black male employers than other respondents. On the other hand, Table 13 reports that the largest percentage of the respondents who prefer Black female employers and worked long hours were social workers (33 percent), nurses (29 percent), administrators (22 percent), clerical workers (14 percent), and domestic workers (13 percent), while Table 14 indicates that, of the respondents who prefer white male employers, the highest percentage that worked long hours were nurses (27 percent), administrators (21 percent), and teachers (14 percent). Even so, the administrators who prefer white female employers and Black male employers had been assigned long work hours more frequently than other respondents. However, there is one exception; white female employers did not assign social workers long hours. Besides, the respondents in social work who prefer female employers were also more likely to be assigned long work hours than other respondents. Again, the administrators who prefer white female employers were excepted.

The Tidewater respondents also reported that after obtaining jobs, they experienced other types of discrimination, such as low wages. They were operationalized as a salary lower then either what they deserved for their work or needed to maintain their household. We found, as shown in Table 11, variation by employer type. The data indicate that 25 percent of the respondents who prefer white female employers, 21 percent who prefer Black male employers, 14 percent who prefer Black female employers, and 13 percent who prefer white male employers received low wages for working more often than other respondents. This analysis also indicates that the white female and Black male employers were more similar, and the Black female and white male employers were more similar than same race employers on this variable. In effect, there was a cross sex principle as well as a transracial principle involved in the receipt of low wages. Of course, there was variation by occupation of respondents. As noted in Table 12, of the respondents who prefer white female employers, the administrators (60 percent), social workers (50 percent), and domestic workers (36 percent) experienced low wages more often than nurses (11 percent), teachers (6 percent), and clerical workers (0 percent). This analysis also indicates that administrators and service type workers received low wages more frequently than all other respondents. Likewise, as seen in Table 15, of the respondents who prefer Black male

43

employers, the social workers (60 percent), administrators (44 percent), nurses (30 percent), and teachers (29 percent) had received low wages more often than clerical (14 percent) and domestic workers (0 percent). Similarly, the respondents who prefer Black female employers varied in their experience with low wages (see Table 13). Thus, more administrators (56 percent), nurses (29 percent), and social workers (17 percent) reported that they had received low wages than domestic workers (13 percent), teachers (6 percent), and clerical workers (7 percent). It should be noted, however, that a larger percentage of administrators and service type workers received low wages than respondents in other occupations. On the other hand, there was less variation, by occupational groups, among respondents who prefer white male employers (Table 14). Of these respondents, this experience was more frequent among social workers (22 percent) than among administrators (14 percent), nurses and clerical workers (each 13 percent), and domestic workers (10 percent). It thus appears that, in general, a larger percentage of administrators and service type workers received lower wages than respondents in other occupations.

That Black women had problems obtaining good wages is indeed evident in these data. Low wages are often a result of the jobs Black women hold. For example, "among all female workers, Negro women thus comprise half or more of the domestics and paid farm workers, one fourth or more of the laundry and dry cleaning operations and charwomen, and one fifth of the cooks and institutional attendents" (Ginzberg and Hiestand 1966:213). Besides, "half of the Negro women in the professional and technical occupations are school teachers, and half of those who are managers and proprietors are in wholesale and retail trade" (Ginzberg and Hiestand 1966:213). Because "black women contribute proportionately more to the Black family's income than white women, the relative importance of working wives' contribution to family income, especially in Black communities, is even greater" (Brimmer 1978:57). Thus, it is important for Black women to obtain higher paying jobs. One way to overcome this barrier is "to set long-range career goals and work toward them through a calculated series of raises and promotions" (Nivens 1978:14). Thus, the achievement of high wages requires Black women to strive to improve their lot by following a planned procedure.

After the respondents received their jobs and wages, some of them did not get a raise. When this variable was crosstabulated with employer types, the results were informative (see Table 11). They indicate that the respondents who prefer working for white male employers (28 percent) received a raise less often than the respondents who prefer working for white female (23 percent) and Black male and female employers (each 17 percent). They also indicate that white employers failed to give the respondents a raise more often than Black employers. Of the respondents who prefer white male employers, it occurred more frequently among the domestic workers (60 percent), social workers (44 percent), nurses (27 percent), and administrators (21 percent) in Table 14. Hence, the employers failed to give respondents in service type occupations a raise more often than other employers. Regarding white female employers, 46 percent of the respondents in domestic work, 33 percent in social work, and 20 percent in administration did not get a raise (see Table 12). Also, both white employers failed to give administrators a raise with about the same frequency. Another finding is that although some Tidewater respondents reached the administrative level of employment, they did not always receive a raise. On the other hand, of the respondents who prefer Black female employers, 29 percent of the clerical workers, 25 percent of the domestic workers, and 17 percent of the social workers failed to get a raise more often than other respondents in Table 13. Similarly, 38 percent of the clerical workers, 25 percent of the domestic workers, and 20 percent of the social workers who prefer Black male employers failed to get a raise more often than other employees in Table 15. Consequently, Black employers tended to give service type workers a raise less often than other employees, but the experience was known most frequently among clerical workers. We also found that more often than not, all employers failed to give service type workers a raise than other respondents.

Of course, some of the respondents had obtained raises on their jobs. The problem that they encountered was getting raises on time (see Table 11). The findings are similar to the preceding variable; thus, 37 percent of the respondents who prefer white female employers, 30 percent who prefer white male employers, 18 percent who prefer Black male employers and 17 percent who prefer Black female employers were likely not to get a raise on time. The data in this table also indicate that the respondents who prefer white employers were more likely not to get a raise on time than respondents who prefer Black employers. Likewise, the respondents who prefer female employers were more likely not to get a raise on time than the respondents who prefer male employers. Given these factors, it appears that the sex and race of the Tidewater employers influenced how often the respondents received raises on time.

The respondents who prefer white employers also varied by occupation in frequency of failure to get a raise on time (see Table 12 and Table 14). Among the respondents who prefer white female employers,

45

it occurred most frequently among domestic workers (64 percent), social workers (50 percent), and nurses (33 percent) while it occurred most often among social workers (67 percent), nurses (40 percent), and clerical workers (21 percent) who prefer white male employers. As a result, white employers failed to give service type workers a raise on time more frequently than other types of workers. We next crosstabulated this variable for all employer types by age of the respondents. However, only the data for white female employers were found significant. As shown in Table 18, 37 percent of the respondents who prefer white female employers agreed that they had not received their raises on time. Of course, a larger percentage of the women over forty than under forty noted this experience, and the relationship between the age and raise on time variables is significant at the .02 level.

Table 18

White Female Employers Failed to Give Black Female
Employees Raises on time by Age of Respondents

Failed to Give Employees Raise On Time	Age of Respondents					
	Under 40		Over 40		Total	
	No.	%	No.	%	No.	%
Agree	20	28.6	20	54.1	40	37.4
Disagree	50	71.4	17	45.9	67	62.6
Total	70	65.4	37	34.6	107	100.0

Corrected Chi Square = 5.67036 with 1 degree of freedom
P < 0.0173

The respondents who prefer Black employers also varied in frequency of raises on time. For example, among the respondents who prefer Black female employers, the domestic workers (38 percent), social workers (33 percent) and teachers (19 percent) failed to get a raise on time more often than other employers who prefer working for them (see Table 13). Similarly, there was variation in this experience among respondents who prefer Black male employers in Table 15. Thus, social workers (40 percent), domestic workers (25 percent), and administrators (22 percent) failed to get a raise on time under Black male employers more often than other respondents who prefer

46

them as employers. Again, as in the case of white employers, service workers were more likely not to get raises on time than other respondents who prefer Black employers. However, in comparing employers, it appears that employees who were administrators had more difficulty getting raises on time from Black male and white female employers than from Black female and white male employers. Since our analysis indicates that some respondents had found it difficult to get raises on time, it seems important that we find ways to overcome this problem. Nivens (1978:14,17,18) has recommended that one way we can achieve a good salary is to research raises and promotions in our places of work, set career goals, and then talk with our supervisor or the person who gives the promotions. This opportunity should be used to let him or her know that our career future in the company is important to us. Such approach would likely help Blacks obtain their raises and promotions on time and employers benefit from greater employee productivity.

The next type of job discrimination that the Tidewater respondents experienced was that they either did not get a promotion or it was overdue (see Table 11). Hence, 27 percent of the respondents who prefer white female employers and 23 percent who prefer Black male employers either did not get promoted or their promotions were overdue. As Table 11 also shows, 21 percent of the respondents who prefer white male employers and 16 percent who prefer Black female employers had faced the same problem. Further, Tables 12-15 indicate that the respondents in some occupations had problems with promotions more often than other respondents. However, of the respondents who prefer Black male, white male, and white female employers, promotions were a problem in all occupational categories. Also, the respondents who prefer Black female employers replicate the pattern of respondents who prefer other employers, but to a lesser extent. It is not enough to identify this problem; Black women must find ways to over come it. For example, Nivens (1978:17) has pointed out that "If (we) want a promotion and (our) company is not locked into granting them based on tenure, (we) must demonstrate that (we) can handle additional responsibilities or that (we) are willing to put in extra effort to learn what we don't know". It thus appears that hard work should be combined with a willingness to learn all that we can to assure job promotion.

Protests Against Job Discrimination

Once we found that Black women in Tidewater experienced job discrimination, the inquiry focused on the reactions of the respondents to

47

problems in the workplace. What we found was that often job discrimination was not protested. For example, a public school teacher in her twenties said:

Because it was my first teaching job, I did not complain about the discrimination. Besides, I did not realize, until after the fact, the extent that I was mistreated. Fortunately, at the end of the term, I was reassigned to another school.

There were also women who did not complain about job discrimination, because they intended to quit their jobs. Then, there were some women who did not complain, because other employees experienced job discrimination long before they were hired. Hence, a nurse in her forties, said:

I have not complained about the discrimination in this hospital, because it was going on before I was hired.

The respondents indicated that, instead of protesting job discrimination, they endured it, quit work, or worked until they could find another job. However, it is likely that the respondents would be more productive if their work environment encouraged them to express their gripes and provided a fair resolution of their problems, because job satisfaction should lead to higher productivity.

That some of the respondents protested job discrimination in the workplace was also evident. The women who prefer all employer types used a variety of protest mechanisms, but the extent each was used varied by employer preferences. One of the protest mechanisms in Table 19 was discussions. Of the respondents who prefer Black male employers, 86 percent used discussions to solve their problems while 66 percent used them to solve their problems with white male employers. On the other hand, 62 percent who prefer white female employers and 55 percent who prefer Black female employers used discussions to resolve differences. Hence, a greater percentage of the women who prefer male employers employed them than women who prefer and work for female employers. This may indicate that Black female employers found it easier to discuss job related problems with male employers than with female employers. On the other hand, a larger percentage of the respondents who prefer Black employers discussed problems related to job discrimination than respondents who prefer white employers.

Table 19 indicates that written complaints were another type of mech-

Table 19

Job Discrimination Protest by Employer Preference

P A N E L	Types of Protest Against Job Discrimination	White Male		Black Male		Black Female		White Female	
		No.	%	No.	%	No.	%	No.	%
A	Discussion:								
	Discussed Job Discrimination With Boss	53	66.2	44	86.3	26	55.3	28	62.2
	Did Not Discuss Job Discrimination With Boss	27	33.8	7	13.7	21	44.7	17	37.8
	Total	80	100.0	51	100.0	47	100.0	45	100.0
B	Formal Complaint:								
	Filed a Formal Complaint	19	24.1	7	14.0	8	17.0	16	35.6
	Did Not File a Formal Complaint	60	75.9	43	86.0	39	83.0	29	64.4
	Total	79	100.0	50	100.0	47	100.0	45	100.0
C	Argument:								
	Argued With Boss	28	35.4	10	20.0	13	27.7	15	33.3
	Did Not Argue With Boss	51	64.6	40	80.0	34	72.3	30	66.7
	Total	79	100.0	50	100.0	47	100.0	45	100.0
D	Attitude:								
	Manifested Unpleasant Attitude	16	20.3	7	14.0	7	14.9	9	20.0
	Did Not Manifest Unpleasant Attitude	63	79.7	43	86.0	40	85.1	36	80.0
	Total	79	100.0	50	100.0	47	100.0	45	100.0
E	Gossip:								
	Gossiped to Fellow Employees About Discrimination	30	38.0	13	26.0	11	23.4	10	22.2
	Did Not Gossip to Fellow Employees About Discrimination	49	62.0	37	74.0	36	76.6	35	77.8
	Total	79	100.0	50	100.0	47	100.0	45	100.0
F	Other:								
	Utilized Other Means of Protest	1	1.2	4	8.0	2	4.3	1	2.2
	Did Not Utilize Other Means of Protest	79	98.8	46	92.0	45	95.7	45	97.8
	Total	80	100.0	50	100.0	47	100.0	46	100.0

Panel E: Black Male
Corrected Chi Square = 4.21761 with 1 degree of freedom
P < 0.0400

anism the Tidewater respondents used to protest discrimination in the workplace. Among the respondents who prefer white female employers, 36 percent had used them to protest discrimination and 24 percent employed them with white male employers while 17 percent of the respondents who prefer Black female employers and 14 percent who prefer Black male employers used written complaints to resolve discriminatory grievances. It thus appears that a larger percentage of the respondents who prefer white employers used written complaints to protest discrimination than respondents who prefer Black employers.

On the other hand, as shown in Table 19, the Tidewater respondents also used arguments to protest discrimination. The respondents who prefer white male employers (35 percent) and white female employers (33 percent) were more likely to argue with their employers about job discrimination than those who prefer Black female employers (28 percent) and Black male employers (20 percent). Hence, white employers were subject more frequently than Black employers to arguments. It is likely that this pattern resulted from a less volatile argument between Blacks and whites than between Blacks and, thus, the respondents were likely to risk arguments with whites more often than with Blacks.

Similarly, Table 19 demonstrates that the Tidewater respondents protested job discrimination by manifesting an unpleasant attitude. It occurred more often with white male and white female employers (each 20 percent) than with Black female (15 percent) and Black male (14 percent) employers. Again, white employers were more likely to experience unpleasant employee attitudes than other employers. It is my hunch that the intensity of unpleasant attitudes was not as great toward whites as toward Blacks, and that unpleasant attitudes were somewhat limited between Blacks, because one misunderstanding could lead to dismissal or quitting and other serious consequences.

Gossip is another pattern of protest against job discrimination in Table 19. The data indicate that the respondents who prefer white male employers (38 percent) and Black male employers (26 percent) gossiped about unfavorable employer actions more frequently than respondents who prefer Black female employers (23 percent) and white female employers (22 percent). Perhaps one possible reason for the frequent use of gossip about male employers was that it resulted in fewer adverse consequences than when they gossiped about female employers. The implication here is that women appear, in some cases, to be more sensitive about adverse behavior than men, yet it is likely that there are men who are more sensitive than women about adverse statements. Another probable reason is that the men, as this study has shown, gave the respondents fewer causes to gossip and, as a result, the respondents probably found it easier to obtain release from less frequent discrimination than from the more frequent discrimination by females. And, as one respondent reported, if discrimination is experienced with a white male employer, she can politely put him in his place and continue working for him. This is likely, though reported by only one respondent, to be a very important point. It is less likely that female employees are able to politely put female employers in their place and continue a satisfactory work relationship. Or, perhaps instead of warmth, Black female employees use harshness

Table 20

Black Female Employees Used Gossip to Protest Job Discrimination
From Black Male Employers by Age of Respondents

Gossiped as A Form of Protest	Age of Respondents					
	Under 40		Over 40		Total	
	No.	%	No.	%	No.	%
Agree	6	16.7	7	50.0	13	26.0
Disagree	30	83.3	7	50.0	37	74.0
Total	36	72.0	14	28.0	50	100.0

Corrected Chi Square = 4.21761 with 1 degree of freedom
P < 0.0400

to adjust differences between themselves and their female employers. If this is the case, employees can reap benefits by using the same tone of approach with female employers as they use with male employers. This matter appears important enough for Black female employees to change their approach and for female employers to allow their actions to be correctly questioned and corrected. This can only result in a higher quality of life in the workplace as well as higher productivity and longevity of employment. Further analysis of these data shows in Table 20 that 50 percent of the women who gossiped about Black male employers were over forty years of age, and the alpha value (.04) indicates a significant relationship between the age of respondents and use of gossip as a protest mechanism with male employers.

Job Satisfaction Derived from Protest to Employers

That the women received some satisfaction in all areas of protest is evident, however, only the findings for Black employers on the job satisfaction variable are significant in Table 21. This table also indicates that there was some variation by employer preference; for example, of the respondents who prefer white male employers, there were a number of changes in their work situation. They received a better attitude (25 percent), fewer demeaning duties (19 percent), a decreased work load (18 percent), a promotion (13 percent), and a shorter work period (10 percent). On the other hand, they also experienced unpleasant working conditions (24 percent) and harassment (14 percent), operationalized in the interviews as discomfort in work situations. Generally, however, the respondents (94 percent) indicated that there were no other consequences of job protest. That the women who prefer Black male employers realized improvements in the workplace is also evident in Table 21. Thus, they realized an improved attitude (31 percent), received a raise (18 percent), obtained a decrease in work hours, and received a promotion (each 17 percent), and were given a decreased work load and few demeaning duties (each 13 percent). Unlike the employees of white male employers, these respondents did not receive adverse consequences from their protest efforts.

That the respondents who prefer Black female employers also received favorable results from protesting job discrimination is another factor in Table 21. In the order of frequency, they received a smaller work load (18 percent) and realized an enhanced attitude (16 percent), shorter work hours (13 percent), a promotion (11 percent), a raise (7 percent), and fewer demeaning jobs (4 percent). They also received an adverse consequence, harassment (7 percent), from protesting job discrimination.

The data in Table 21 also indicate that the respondents who prefer white female employers reaped some benefits from protesting discrimination. They realized an enhanced attitude (27 percent), less demeaning jobs and a promotion (each 16 percent), a decreased work load (9 percent), and a raise (7 percent). A larger percentage of the respondents received positive benefits from job protest than were received from other employers, yet 16 percent also experienced harassment.

Nevertheless, Table 21 indicates that a large percentage of the respondents who worked for all employers did not receive favorable results from job protest. Failure to obtain results is a type of job harassment that contributes to work discomfort. Therefore, a large percentage of the respondents, who prefer each employer type, experienced harassment by not getting a raise, a reduction in work load and hours and a promotion, as well as results from protest. However, a higher percentage of respondents experienced each type of harassment more frequently with female than male employers. Moreover, female employers failed to give the respondents who prefer working for them raises more often than other employers while Black female and white male employers failed to give the respondents promotions more often than other employers. Also, white female employers failed to decrease the work load and hours more frequently than other employers. Further analysis of these data indicate that, on the basis of the percentage of respondents experiencing the four types of harassment, the order of frequency is: failure to get shorter work hours, a raise, a promotion,

Table 21

Results of Protest Against Job Discrimination by Employer Preference

P a n e l	Results From Protest	Employer Preference							
		White Male		Black Male		Black Female		White Female	
		No.	%	No.	%	No.	%	No.	%
A	**Raise:**								
	Given Raise	15	18.8	9	18.4	3	6.5	3	6.8
	Was Not Given Raise	65	81.2	40	81.6	43	93.5	41	93.2
	Total	80	100.0	49	100.0	46	100.0	44	100.0
B	**Job Type:**								
	Given Less Demeaning Jobs	15	18.8	6	12.5	2	4.4	7	15.9
	Was Not Given Less Demeaning Jobs	65	81.2	42	87.5	43	95.6	37	84.1
	Total	80	100.0	48	100.0	45	100.0	44	100.0
C	**Work Load:**								
	Decreased Work Load	14	17.5	6	12.5	8	17.8	4	9.1
	Did Not Receive Decreased Work Load	66	82.5	42	87.5	37	82.2	40	90.9
	Total	80	100.0	48	100.0	45	100.0	44	100.0
D	**Work Period:**								
	Decrease in Hours Worked	8	10.0	8	16.7	6	13.3	2	4.5
	No Decrease in Hours Worked	72	90.0	40	83.3	39	86.7	42	95.5
	Total	80	100.0	48	100.0	45	100.0	44	100.0
E	**Promotion:**								
	Received a Promotion	10	12.5	8	16.7	5	11.1	7	15.9
	Did Not Receive a Promotion	70	87.5	40	83.3	40	88.9	37	84.1
	Total	80	100.0	48	100.0	45	100.0	44	100.0
F	**Attitude:**								
	Enhanced Attitude	20	25.0	15	31.2	7	15.6	12	27.3
	Did Not Enhance Attitude	60	75.0	33	68.8	38	84.4	32	72.7
	Total	80	100.0	48	100.0	45	100.0	44	100.0
G	**Harassment:**								
	Received Harassment	11	13.7	5	10.4	3	6.8	7	15.9
	Did Not Receive Harassment	69	86.3	43	89.6	41	93.2	37	84.1
	Total	80	100.0	48	100.0	44	100.0	44	100.0
H	**Work Situation:**								
	Work Situation Became Unpleasant	19	24.1	7	14.6	7	16.7	8	18.2
	Work Situation Did Not Become Unpleasant	60	75.9	41	85.4	35	83.3	36	81.8
	Total	79	100.0	48	100.0	42	100.0	44	100.0
I	**Other Results:**								
	Protest Caused Other Consequences	5	6.3	1	2.1	5	11.6	3	6.8
	Protest Did Not Cause Other Consequences	75	93.8	47	97.9	38	88.4	41	93.2
	Total	80	100.0	48	100.0	43	100.0	44	100.0

Panel B: Black Male
    Corrected Chi Square = 6.97239 with 1 degree of freedom
    P < 0.0083
  Black Female
    Corrected Chi Square = 3.95712 with 1 degree of freedom
    P < 0.0467

and a lighter work load. Moreover, the data show that the respondents received less harassment from Black employers about promotions and work hours while they received less harassment for raises from white male employers.

Protest to Supervisors of Immediate Employers

Not only did the respondents complain to their immediate supervisors, but they also complained to the supervisors of their employers (see Table 22). For example, a nurse in her thirties complained to the Black supervisor of her immediate employer. She gave the following account of this complaint:

Because I am outspoken, my supervisor always gave me a below average evaluation. For example, my nursing supervisor saw me as a threat and used one incident to complain about me on my yearly evaluation. I took my complaint to the floor director of nursing and told her that if my immediate supervisor felt that she could not communicate with me, it was her duty, during the course of the year, to call both of us in and find out why. Our problems began after I had worked two years and found that my immediate supervisor had recommended that I receive the same pay as a beginning nurse.

As noted in Table 22, a larger percentage of the Tidewater respondents complained to the supervisors of Black employers than to supervisors of white employers. The order of frequency that respondents complained to supervisors of their immediate employers is: Black female (44 percent), white female (25 percent), white male (24 percent), and Black male (21 percent). In effect, complaints to immediate employers and their supervisors had an adverse effect on the respondents' job satisfaction in the workplace.

Table 22

Results of Protest Against Job Discrimination to Supervisor
of Immediate Employer by Employer
Preference

P A N E L	Complained To Supervisors About Bosses' Job Discrimination	Employer Preference							
		White Male		Black Male		Black Female		White Female	
		Agree	Disagree	Agree	Disagree	Agree	Disagree	Agree	Disagree
		No %	No %	No %	No %	No %	No %	No %	No %
A	Complained To Supervisors of White Male Employers	10 23.8	32 76.2						
B	Complained To Supervisors of Black Male Employers			6 21.4	22 78.6				
C	Complained To Supervisors of Black Female Employers					7 43.8	9 56.2		
D	Complained To Supervisors of White Female Employers							4 25.0	12 75.0

54

Justice in Protest Complaints

When race of supervisors of the respondents in this Tidewater study was crosstabulated with age, there was only a slight difference in the number of women who received justice in their discrimination complaints in Table 23. Hence, Black supervisors of employers gave about the same amount of justice in complaints as white supervisors. Nevertheless, stressful work relations led some of the Tidewater respondents to take their job protests to the supervisor of their immediate employer to enhance their job satisfaction.

Table 23

Justice Received From Job Discrimination Complaints
by Race of Employer's Supervisor

P a n e l	Justice	Supervisor of Employers by Race			
		White Supervisors of Bosses		Black Supervisor of Bosses	
		No.	%	No.	%
A	Awarded More Justice	41	37.3	39	41.1
B	Was Not Awarded More Justice	69	62.7	56	58.9
	Total	110	100.0	95	100.0

55

REFERENCES CITED

Alexis, Marcus
    1974   "The Political Economy of Labor Market Discrimination: Synthesis and Exploration." In A. Horowitz and G. VonFurstenberg (eds.) PATTERNS OF DISCRIMINATION, Vol. II. Lexington: D. C. Heath Co., pp. 63-83.

Ash, Philip
    1972   "Job Satisfaction Differences among Women of Different Ethnic Groups," THE JOURNAL OF VOCATIONAL BEHAVIOR 4:495-50.

Barnes, Annie S.
    1977   "The Economic and Social Structure of the Atlanta Community," JOURNAL OF SOCIAL AND BEHAVIORAL SCIENCES 238:353-360.

Beal, Frances M.
    1975   "Slave of a Slave No More: Black Women in Struggle." THE BLACK SCHOLAR 6:2-10.

Becker, Gary
    1957   THE ECONOMICS OF DISCRIMINATION. Chicago: The University of Chicago Press.

Billingsley, Andrew T.
    1968   BLACK FAMILIES IN WHITE AMERICA. Englewood CLiffs: Prentice-Hall, Inc.

Blubaugh, Jon A. and Dorothy L. Pennington
    1976   CROSSING DIFFERENCE. . .INTERRACIAL COMMUNICATION. Columbus: Charles E. Merrill Publishing Company.

Boggs, James
    1972   "Blacks in the Cities: Agenda for the 70s." The BLACK SCHOLAR 4:50-61.

Brimmer, Andrew
1978 "Economic Perspectives." BLACK ENTERPRISE 9:57.

Brimmer, Andrew
1978 "Economic Perspectives." BLACK ENTERPRISE 9:120.

Carvell, Fred J.
1970 HUMAN RELATIONS IN BUSINESS. New York: The MacMillan Company.

Champagne, Joseph E. and Donald C. King
1967 "Job Satisfaction Factors Among Underprivileged Workers." THE PERSONNEL AND GUIDANCE JOURNAL 5:429-434.

Chisholm, Shirley
1970 "Racism and Anti-Feminism." THE BLACK SCHOLAR 3-4:40-45.

Feagin, Joe R. and Clairece Booher Feagin
1978 DISCRIMINATION AMERICAN STYLE (Institutional Racism and Sexism). Englewood Cliffs: Prentice-Hall, Inc.

Friedlander, Frank and Stuart Greenberg
1971 "Effect of Job Attitudes, Training, and Organization Climate on Performance of the Hard Core Unemployed." APPLIED PSYCHOLOGY 4:287-295.

Gibson, D. Parke
1978 "Money: How We Earn It and How We Spend It." The BLACK COLLEGIAN 9:20,22.

Ginzberg, Eli and Dale E. Hiestand
1966 "Employment Patterns of Negro Men and Women." In John P. Davis (ed.) THE AMERICAN NEGRO REFERENCE BOOK. Englewood Cliffs: Prentice-Hall, Inc.

Greenhaus, Jeffrey H. and James F. Gavin
1972 "The Relationship Between Expectancies and Job Behavior for White and Black Employees." PERSONNEL PSYCHOLOGY 3:449-455

Gurin, Patricia
1977 "The Role of Worker Expectancies in the Study of Employment Discrimination." In Phyllis A. Wallace and Annette

M. Lamond (eds.) WOMEN, MINORITIES AND EMPLOY-
MENT DISCRIMINATION. Lexington: D. C. Heath & Co.,
pp. 13-37.

Hill, Herbert
1977   "Postponement of Economic Equality." THE BLACK
SCHOLAR 9:18-23.

Hood, Elizabeth F.
1978   "Black Women, White Women: Separate Paths to Liberation."
THE BLACK SCHOLAR 9:45-46.

Krueger, Ann
1963   "The Economics of Discrimination." JOURNAL OF POLITI-
CAL ECONOMY.

Lefcourt, Herbert M. and Gordon W. Ladwig
1965   "The American Negro: A Problem in Expectancies." JOUR-
NAL OF PERSONALITY AND SOCIAL PSYCHOLOGY
2:377-380.

Lefton, Mark
1968   "Race Expectancies and Anomie." SOCIAL FORCES 46:347-
352.

Maier, Norman R.F.
1965   PSYCHOLOGY IN INDUSTRY. Boston: Houghton Mifflin
Company.

Marshall, Ray
1977   "Black Employment in the South." In Phyllis A. Wallace
and Annett M. Lamond (eds.) WOMEN, MINORITIES, AND
EMPLOYMENT DISCRIMINATION. Lexington: D. C. Heath
and Company, pp. 57-81.

Munford, C. J.
1972   "Social Structure and Black Revolution." cf. Veronica F.
Nieva and Barbara A. Gutek, WOMEN AND WORK. New
York: Praeger.

Murphy, Betty
1971   "From Janitor to Manager." OPPORTUNITY 1:30-33.

Nivens, Beatryce
1978   "Raises and Promotions: How to Get What You Deserve."
        ESSENCE :14,17,18.

Nunez, Elizabeth
1974   "Why Black Johnny Can't Write College English." THE
        BLACK SCHOLAR 6:16-18.

Pressman, Sonia
1970   "Job Discrimination and the Black Woman." CRISES 3:103-08

Reed, Julia
1970   "Marriage and Fertility in Black Female Teachers." THE
        BLACK SCHOLAR 1:22-28.

Slocum, John W. and Robert H. Strawser
1972   "Racial Differences in Job Attitudes." JOURNAL OF
        APPLIED PSYCHOLOGY 1:28-32.

Smith, Stanley Hugh
1953   FREEDOM TO WALK. New York: Vantage Press, Inc.

Staff
1961   "What Are The Branches Doing?" CRISES 68:112-116.

Vontress, Clemmont E.
1971   "The Black Male Personality." THE BLACK SCHOLAR
        2:10-16.

Walker, Lynn
1973   "On Employment Discrimination." ESSENCE 4:24.

Weaver, Charles N.
1974   "Negro-White Differences in Job Satisfaction." BUSINESS
        HORIZONS 1:67-72.

Welch, Finish
1967   "Labor-Market Discrimination: An Interpretation of Income
        Differences in the Rural South." THE JOURNAL OF POLIT-
        ICAL ECONOMY 75:225-240.

Welch, Finis
1973   "Educational & Racial Discrimination." In Orley Ashenfelt and
        Albert Rees (eds.) DISCRIMINATION IN LABOR MARKETS.
        Princeton: Princeton University Press.

Wernimont, Paul F.
1964   "Intrinsic and Extrinsic Factors in Job Satisfaction." JOUR-
        NAL OF APPLIED PSYCHOLOGY 50:41-50.

Wesley, Charles H.
1960   "Background and Achievement for Negro Americans." CRISES
        67:133-149.

Williams, J. Sherwood et al.
1974   "Blacks and Southern Poverty." JOURNAL OF SOCIAL
        AND BEHAVIORAL SCIENCES 20:62-71.

1961   "What the Branches are Doing?" CRISES 68:112-116.

U. S. Department of Labor
1969   THE ATLANTA URBAN EMPLOYMENT SURVEY, July,
        1968-June, 1969. Atlanta: Bureau of Labor Statistics,
        p. 8.

CHAPTER THREE

THE BLACK WOMAN IN THE HOME

Because the Black family has its roots in indentured life and slavery, work has always been "the basic economic function for the survival of the black family" (Nelson 1975:11). The first Blacks were brought to America in 1619 as indentured servants (Russell 1913:29) and were the basis for the slave family (Frazier 1932:1). Since slavery was essentially an economic system (Starobin 1970:6), the families raised cotton, tobacco, hemp, sugar, and rice (Starobin 1970:5), cut timber, extracted turpentine, and did domestic work (Stampp 1963:330). The urban slave families were also well acquainted with the workplace. According to Starobin (1970:9,14,19), they worked as "artisans and craftsmen, stevedores and draymen, barbers, common laborers and house and hotel servants." They also worked in manufacturing industries, including tobacco, cotton, and textile factories and made brogans and operated tanneries, bakeries, and paper factories. Nevertheless, extensive participation in the slave system did not improve their living conditions. As also noted by Starobin (1970:57), typically, the industrial slaves lived in cabins, shanties, shacks, or tenements while plantation farmers lived in cabins, and the domestics lived in the "big house" (Stampp 1963:20).

Following the lead of the literature of the slave family, we determined whether modern Black families in Tidewater experience satisfying living conditions. The answer to this inquiry was obtained by asking the Tidewater respondents, on the basis of perceived harshness, to rank seven types of behavior. As Table 1 indicates, our survey confirmed our findings in Chapter 2. Low income, low prestige (demeaning) jobs, and job discrimination were perceived by the Tidewater respondents as relatively harsh types of behavior. As would be expected, low income was harsher on respondents under than over forty years of age while job discrimination was more difficult for women over forty. It is also important to note that though both age groups ranked racism as one of the harshest types of behavior, income and jobs

61

Table 1

Harsh Experiences of Respondents by Age

Panel	Harsh Experiences	Age of Respondents					
		Under 40		Over 40		Total	
		%	Rank	%	Rank	%	Rank
A	Low Income	64.5	1	55.6	2	61.7	1
B	Low Prestige Jobs	60.1	2	57.1	1	59.2	2
C	Racism	57.2	3	47.6	3	54.2	3
D	Large Families	52.2	5	46.0	5	50.2	4
E	Sex Discrimination	55.1	4	36.5	6	49.3	5
F	Out of Wedlock Births	41.3	7	47.6	4	43.3	6
G	Unkind Treatment by Spouses	50.0	6	27.0	7	42.8	7
H	Unkind Treatment by Other Black Women	37.2	8	17.5	8	31.0	8

$$\text{Spearman rho} = \frac{P - 1}{N} \times \frac{6 \ D^2}{(N-1)^2} = +0.79$$

Panel E: Corrected Chi Square = 5.24452 with 1 degree of freedom
P < 0.0220
Panel G: Corrected Chi Square = 8.44337 with 1 degree of freedom
P < 0.0037
Panel H: Corrected Chi Square = 6.98537 with 1 degree of freedom
P < 0.0082

were more crucial to the respondents. As further indicated in Chapter 2, low income and low prestige jobs were related to job discrimination. The finding that low income was a problem among the Tidewater respondents is also suggested in Table 1, Chapter 1. As can be seen from this table, the income of the respondents, in 1979, ranged from over $19,000 to less than $4,000, and the median range was below the nonfarm poverty level, $6,650 per year for a family of four. Hence, 115 or more than half of the 228 respondents who specified their income earned less than $7,000 annually.

We next used the chi square test of significance to determine whether each of the perceived harsh experiences in Table 1 is statistically significant by age of respondents. Unlike other crosstabulations, we found that age is significantly related to the harsh perceptions that the respondents held toward sex discrimination and unkind treatment by spouses and other Black women, but they were harsher on the respondents under forty than over forty years of age. By using Spearman rho, we also determined that there is a high correlation between age and all the data in Table 1, including insufficient income.

Table 2

Insufficient Income Is A Problem among Black Women
by Annual Income of Respondents

Annual Income of	Insufficient Income is a Problem											
	Strongly Agree		Agree		No Opinion		Disagree		Strongly Disagree		Total	
	No.	%	No.	%	No.	%	No.	%	No.	%	No.	%
25,000-49,999	0	0.0	1	100.0	0	0.0	0	0.0	0	0.0	1	100.0
22,000-24,999	1	25.0	1	25.0	0	0.0	2	50.0	0	0.0	4	100.0
19,000-21,999	2	50.0	1	25.0	0	0.0	1	25.0	0	0.0	4	100.0
16,000-18,999	1	16.7	3	50.0	1	16.7	1	16.7	0	0.0	6	100.0
13,000-15,999	9	47.4	9	47.4	0	0.0	1	5.2	0	0.0	19	100.0
10,000-12,999	11	45.8	10	41.7	0	0.0	3	12.5	0	0.0	24	100.0
7,000-9,999	28	54.9	22	43.1	0	0.0	1	2.0	0	0.0	51	100.0
4,000-6,999	16	53.3	9	30.0	2	6.7	2	6.7	1	3.3	30	100.0
3,999 or less	16	59.3	8	29.6	1	3.7	1	3.7	1	3.7	27	100.0
Desire No Work	2	33.3	4	66.7	0	0.0	0	0.0	0	0.0	6	100.0
Desire Work-No Job	3	23.1	7	53.8	3	23.1	0	0.0	0	0.0	13	100.0
Retired	4	33.3	2	16.7	1	8.3	5	41.7	0	0.0	12	100.0
Public Assist.	14	73.7	5	26.3	0	0.0	0	0.0	0	0.0	19	100.0
Housewife	6	75.0	2	25.0	0	0.0	0	0.0	0	0.0	8	100.0

Corrected Chi Square = 25.24140 with 12 degrees of freedom
P > 0.0137

Because low income was ranked number one by the respondents under forty and number two by the respondents over forty, as one of the harsh experiences, we pursued the income question in greater detail. As shown in Table 2, although some of them had a sizeable income, a large percentage of each income category either agreed or strongly agreed that insufficient income was a problem among Black women in Tidewater. Another finding in this table is that a significant relationship exists between income categories and the view that insufficient income was a problem among Black women in Tidewater. However, there is some differentiation in the frequency of this variable by income level. For example, 100 percent of the respondents earning $25,000-$49,999, receiving public assistance, serving as homemakers, or desiring not to work agreed that insufficient income is a problem among Black women in Tidewater. Further analysis of the data, as indicated in Table 3, shows that 205 of the 233 respondents, who gave their age and answered this question, agreed that lack of sufficient income is a problem, but there is not much difference between the percentage of women under forty (89 percent) compared to the percentage of women over forty (85 percent) with this opinion.

Perhaps inadequate income is related to certain problems, including

Table 3

Insufficient Income is a Problem among Black Women
by Age of Respondents

Insufficient	Age of Respondents					
Income is	Under 40		Over 40		Total	
a Problem	No.	%	No.	%	No.	%
Agree	141	89.2	64	85.3	205	88.0
Disagree	12	7.6	8	10.7	20	8.6
No opinion	5	3.2	3	4.0	8	3.4
Total	158	67.8	75	32.2	233	100.0

poor housing. In this regard, the respondents reported that housing in Tidewater does not provide adequate space for doing school homework, eating, sleeping, privacy, and storage of possessions. This finding is supported by Willie (1970:13) who stated that almost half of the Blacks in the south and 16 percent in the north and west live in substandard housing. On the other hand, according to Drake and Cayton (1945:663), home ownership was a consuming passion in Chicago and there was "a tendency for the upper and middle class families to become segregated in the better areas of the Negro community." Atlanta is very similar to Chicago in that Black middle class families live mainly in well-manicured neighborhoods in southwest and northwest Atlanta. In 1970, for example, the families in Golden Towers, a neighborhood in northwest Atlanta, lived in homes that had an assessed tax value between $18,200 and $69,125 (Barnes 1971:71). Nevertheless, for a majority of us, "low income and size of family quite naturally magnify the housing plight of Blacks and the situation is further exacerbated by the fact that Blacks have been categorically denied the opportunity to attain home ownership" (Hawkins 1976:78).

It is burdensome to lack adequate income and housing. As a result, we decided to determine the quality of marriage relations in Black household settings. A major question in this pioneering approach to the study of Black marriages was what ways husbands posed problems for their wives and the reactions of Black women to such problems

Table 4

Husbands Treat Wives Unkindly
by Age of Respondents

	Age of Respondents					
Response	Under 40		Over 40		Total	
	No.	%	No.	%	No.	%
Agree	118	90.1	63	92.6	181	91.0
Disagree	13	9.9	5	7.4	18	9.0
Total	131	65.8	68	34.2	199	100.0

and its effect on them. To find the answer to the initial question, we asked the respondents whether they perceived Black marriages in Tidewater as stressful, operationalized as unkind treatment of wives by husbands. We find from Table 4 that 91 percent of the women in this sample agreed that it was a major problem among Tidewater women while 9 percent of the respondents disagreed that Tidewater wives encountered unkind husband treatment. The findings indicate that there were problems in Tidewater marriages. They were supported in a 1975 study comprised of 49 Black women and 39 Black men, conducted by Rodgers-Rose (1980:258), which indicated negative qualities and behaviors that each disliked in the other. However, Rodgers-Rose (1980:258) found "that women were able to list more negative qualities disliked in males than vice versa." Due to the sensitivity of such questions, as mentioned in Chapter 1, we sometimes asked the Tidewater respondents to talk about the relations that women they knew had with their husbands.

Wife and Husband Employment

We turn now to a categorical description of the marital relations of the respondents and other Black women in Tidewater. The categories of marital behavior employed to describe their behavior are employment, paychecks, decision making, mechanical knowledge, and emotional behavior. Employment, as used here, denotes that Black husbands and wives worked, and this analysis is begun with the employment of the 148 married respondents. They were asked how their husbands

TABLE 5

Reactions of Husbands to Working Wives
by Age of Respondents

Panel	Reactions	Under 40 No.	Under 40 %	Over 40 No.	Over 40 %	Total No.	Total %
A	Husbands Desired Wives to Work	47	60.3	35	60.3	82	60.3
	Husbands Did Not Desire Wives to Work	31	39.7	23	39.7	54	39.7
	Total	78	57.4	58	42.6	136	100.0
B	Husbands Liked For Wives to Get Good Paying Jobs	53	65.4	37	62.7	90	64.3
	Husbands Did Not Like For Wives to Get Good Paying Jobs	28	34.6	22	37.3	50	35.7
	Total	81	57.9	59	42.1	140	100.0
C	Husbands Liked to See Wives Get Promoted	63	79.7	49	84.5	112	81.8
	Husbands Did Not Like to See Wives Get Promoted	16	20.3	9	15.5	25	18.2
	Total	79	57.7	58	42.3	137	100.0

reacted to their employment and their responses were crosstabulated with their age. As noted in Table 5, 60 percent of the respondents over and under forty said that their husbands desired them to work. Thus, for the most part, the husbands of the respondents were favorable toward their employment. The Tidewater women often worked because the money was needed, a finding supported by Brimmer (1978) in Chapter 2. It seems to infer that, when Black women earn low wages, family income is likely to be depressed. According to the respondents, this was precisely the problem that caused stress in their marriages, because they preferred working by choice rather than need.

A related question was whether the husbands of Tidewater respondents desired their wives to receive high wages. The data in Table 5 indicate that 64 percent of the spouses of the respondents liked for them to receive good paying jobs. Likewise, as noted in Table 5, 82 percent of the respondents were married to husbands who liked to see them get promoted, but a larger percentage of the women over forty than under forty were married to men favorable toward their promotions. Further, this is the only variable in Table 5 that indicates important variation by age of respondents and attitudes of their husbands toward them working.

Although a large percentage of the respondents preferred working

Table 6

Relationship Between Intrinsic Work Satisfaction
and Age of Respondents

Panel	Intrinsic Satisfaction	Under 40 No.	%	Over 40 No.	%	No	%
A	Prefer Working to Staying At Home	130	86.1	55	83.3	185	85.3
	Did Not Prefer Working to Staying At Home	21	13.9	11	16.7	32	14.7
	Total	151	69.6	66	30.4	217	100.0
B	Work to Prevent Boredom	51	34.2	8	11.3	59	26.8
	Did Not Work to Prevent Boredom	98	65.8	63	88.7	161	73.2
	Total	149	67.7	81	32.3	220	100.0
C	Work to Obtain Inspiration For Homemaking	23	15.4	13	13.3	36	16.4
	Did Not Work to Obtain Inspiration For Homemaking	126	84.6	58	81.7	184	83.6
	Total	149	67.7	71	32.3	220	100.0
D	Work to Enhance Esteem	120	78.4	43	62.3	163	73.4
	Did Not Work to Enhance Esteem	33	21.6	26	37.7	59	26.6
	Total	153	68.9	69	31.1	222	100.0
E	Work Makes Respondents Feel Less Feminine	12	7.7	5	7.0	17	7.5
	Work Did Not Make Respondents Feel Less Feminine	144	92.3	66	93.0	210	92.5
	Total	156	68.7	71	31.3	227	100.0
F	Leads to Guilty Feeling	13	8.2	8	11.3	21	9.1
	Did Not Lead to Guilty Feeling	146	91.8	63	88.7	209	90.9
	Total	159	69.1	71	30.9	230	100.0

Panel B: Corrected Chi Square = 11.77339 with 1 degree of freedom
P < 0.0006
Panel D: Corrected Chi Square = 5.52799 with 1 of freedeom
P < 0.0187

by choice, rather than need, they still derived intrinsic satisfaction in the workplace. Table 6 presents the varied types of intrinsic satisfaction that the respondents received from working. However, only two types, prevention of boredom (.00) and enhancement of self esteem (.02), are statistically significant, but all types of satisfaction are insightful. Hence, the data in Table 6 indicate that 85 percent of the respondents preferred working to staying at home, and 27 percent of them worked to keep from getting bored, but a larger percentage of the respondents under forty (34 percent) than over forty (11 percent) worked to keep from getting bored. This table is also informative, for it indicates that the notion of being bored as a result of staying at home is not widespread among the Tidewater respondents. As also noted in Table 6, an even smaller percentage (16 percent) of the women worked to get inspiration to perform their homemaking duties. The percentages for both variables for younger as well as older women were expectedly small, because as mentioned earlier, economic need was the primary reason that a large percentage of the women worked. On the other hand, almost three fourths of the respondents reported that working made them feel good about themselves in Table 6; the relationship between the two variables is significant at the .02 level. However, a relatively large percentage (73 percent) of the respondents in both age categories agreed that working made them feel good about themselves, yet a larger percentage of the women under forty (78 percent) than over forty (62 percent) agreed that a career contributed to their self image. Of course, as shown in Table 6, only 8 percent of the respondents reported that working made them feel less feminine while 9 percent of the respondents stated that they felt guilty about working. Both of these findings seem to indicate that employment outside the home is an expected type of behavior in the respondents' marriages.

Because the husbands of the Tidewater respondents were favorable toward their employment, it follows that they received extrinsic satisfaction, as well, from working. Table 7 presents the types of extrinsic satisfaction that they received. The largest percentage reported that a job contributed to their economic security (72 percent) and gave them money to support their household (66 percent). There is some variation by age on both variables; for example, a larger percentage of younger than older respondents worked to enhance their economic security and support their household while 50 percent of the respondents also worked to obtain purchases for themselves and their homes. Another reason that the respondents (38 percent) worked was to educate their children, but a larger percentage of the women in Table 7 over forty (49 percent) than under forty (32 percent) agreed that they worked for this reason; moreover, the relationship between the age of the respondents and working to educate their children is significant at the .02 level.

It is interesting, however, that only 25 percent of the respondents in Table 7 worked to obtain money for recreation. This may indicate that the respondents' recreation was often family oriented. In reviewing the literature on Black family behavior, two factors stand out; one is that most families chose noncommercial recreation. For example, the slave families spent their leisure time relaxing, attending corn shuckings, and persimmon parties, reciting folklore, singing spirituals, dancing, hunting, trapping, and fishing (Stampp 1963:364-367). On the other hand, a second factor about Black family

Table 7

Relationship Between Extrinsic Work Satisfaction
And Age of Respondents

P A N E L	Extrinsic Satisfaction	Age of Respondents					
		Under 40		Over 40		Total	
		No.	%	No.	%	No.	%
A	Work Contributes to Economic Security	111	72.5	48	69.6	159	71.6
	Work Did Not Contribute to Economic Security	42	27.5	21	30.4	63	28.4
	Total	153	68.9	69	31.1	222	100.0
B	Work Produces Household Money	103	69.1	43	60.6	146	66.4
	Work Did Not Produce Household Money	46	30.9	28	39.4	74	33.6
	Total	149	67.7	71	32.3	220	100.0
C	Work Provides Money For Personal and Household Shopping	76	51.0	33	46.5	109	49.5
	Work Did Not Provide Money For Personal and Household Shopping	73	49.0	38	53.5	111	50.5
	Total	149	67.7	71	32.3	220	100.0
D	Work Helps Educate Children	48	32.2	35	49.3	83	37.7
	Work Did Not Help Educate Children	101	67.8	36	50.7	137	62.3
	Total	149	67.7	71	32.3	220	100.0
E	Work Helps Accumulate Savings	51	34.5	17	23.9	68	31.1
	Work Did Not Help Accumulate Saving	97	65.5	54	76.1	151	68.9
	Total	148	67.6	71	32.4	219	100.0
F	Work Produces Recreation Money	37	24.8	18	25.4	55	25.0
	Work Did Not Produce Recreation Money	112	75.2	53	74.6	156	75.0
	Total	149	67.7	71	32.3	211	100.0

Panel D: Corrected Chi Square = 5.26676 with 1 degree of freedom
P < 0.0217

recreation is that middle class families sometimes engage in activities that require money. Because of segregation and relatively high wages, the Black bourgeoisie engaged in a number of activities with each other that required economic support. For example, Frazier (1957:203, 204,212) has noted that the "society" segment of the bourgeoisie attended debutante balls, engaged in conspicuous consumption, and attended fraternity and sorority activities. They also played cards, drank, went to movies and parties, played poker, and participated in voluntary associations (Frazier 1957:47). Moreover, Frazier (1957:229) has also noted that the "society" families created a fantasy world as "a shield from the harsh economic and social realities of American life." It was "created out of the myth of Negro business, the reports of the Negro press on the achievements and wealth of

69

Negro society." Emphasis was placed on "playing seriously" rather than working seriously (Frazier 1957:205); nevertheless, it did not eliminate feelings of insecurity, frustration, and guilt (Frazier 1957:232). However, another segment of the bourgeoisie that resided in Durham, North Carolina was industrious, morally upright and frugal, and abstemious in their habits (Frazier 1957:125) while a third segment of the bourgeoisie took their work seriously and lived in relative obscurity from the Negro world (Frazier 1957:229). It thus appears that the Black bourgeoise depended on their family as well as society for recreation.

The modern lower class offers a contrast to the Black bourgeoisie. As an example, in Spout Spring, a low income Black neighborhood in Sequoyah, recreation is relatively inexpensive. The men gather at Grant's Tavern daily, Sunday excepted, to talk about jobs, cars, women, politics, personalities, sports, and business deals (Kunkel and Kennard 1971:16). It appears that they achieve prestige and self esteem by talking, arguing, fighting, dancing, and shooting pool while the women often receive catharsis in the home, school, and church (Kunkel and Kennard 1971:15). Similarly, in Holmes County, Mississippi, adult family members get together at church and in the home of a family member at least once a month (Shimkin 1978:108). On the other hand, the modern Black middle class is a mixture of the bourgeoisie and lower income family. Their recreation, in Atlanta, for example, is centered around playing bridge, attending social club meetings, going to church, engaging in family activities, attending parties, and visiting relatives (Barnes 1983:67-68); thus, recreation is centered in family activities as well as in community life.

As can also be seen in Table 7, essentials basic to their livelihood consume most of the Tidewater respondents' income and, therefore, less than a third of them work to accumulate savings. These findings support the respondents' desire for their husbands to work and bring their paycheck home. Black men in all social classes earned paychecks to help support their household. For example, as Frazier has noted: in the 1950s, some members of the bourgeoisie were self employed while the majority were employed in the wider society. The occupational and economic position of this latter group was influenced by segregation. Nevertheless, their occupational affiliations included professional, technical, managerial, administrative, proprietal, clerical, sales, craftsmen and foremen's work (Frazier 1957:47). Although the latter two groups were in the lower middle class, Frazier (1957:50, 52) included them in the Black bourgeoisie, however, the entire group was essentially white collar workers.

Black men in the modern low income group also worked to support their family. For example, in the community of Spout Spring in Sequoyah, a majority of the Black low income families earned annual incomes below $5,000 mainly in unskilled and semiskilled jobs in the community (Kunkel and Kennard 1971:129). Similar to the slave and Black bourgeoisie family, discrimination was a major determinant of their relatively low income status (Miller 1964:140-153).

Not unlike the slave, low income, and Black bourgeoisie families, the modern middle class husbands also worked to support their family. They, too, earned their livelihood mainly in the wider society; an example is the residents in Golden Towers, a neighborhood in Northwest Atlanta, Georgia. In 1970, they were employed in service (2.5 percent), blue collar (15.0 percent), white collar (26.3 percent), and professional (46.2 percent) occupations" (Barnes 1983:58,60). According to Barnes (1983:60), from their work, the spouses and widows received a combined annual income that ranged from the $10,000-$13,999 category to over $50,000, but the most frequently earned combined income was between $14,000 and $21,999, and the average household income was $25,207.90."

Table 8

Annual Money Income of Families Living in The City of Atlanta
July, 1968—June, 1969

Norm and Income Bracket	Number	$	Total %	Percentages Negro %	White &
Total families	111,400				
Negro	50,200				
White	61,300				
Total median income		7,600			
Negro		5,900			
White		9,000			
Income bracket($)					
---3,499			15.9	24.1	11.6
3,500 to 4,999			12.5	15.8	8.6
5,000 t0 7,999			24.3	27.7	21.4
8,000 to 9,999			14.3	12.6	15.3
10,000 or more			32.0	18.8	43.1

Families of two or more in City of Atlanta
Sic
Source: U.S. Department of Labor Statistics, THE ATLANTA URBAN EMPLOYMENT
SURVEY, JULY, 1958–JUNE 1969. Atlanta Georgia: Southern Regional
Office, 1969, p.14.

71

However, there are other findings about the economic life of Black families in Atlanta. For example, the data in Table 8 make it possible to compare the earnings of Black families and white families in Atlanta. It is seen that 19 percent of the Black families in Atlanta earned $10,000 or more while 43 percent of the white families equalled or exceeded a $10,000 annual income (Barnes 1977:356). As also found in Table 8, the percentage of white families with very low income (under $3,000) was 12 percent while 24 percent of the Black families lived on the same amount of income. Thus, Black families were more heavily concentrated in the lower end of income distribution (Barnes 1977:356). Billingsley (1968:88) has explained this finding by noting that independently of the ability of Negro workers, "discrimination in the opportunity structure "limits their earning potential and income."

Table 9

Husband Failure to Bring Paycheck Home Effects
Marriage Relations by Age of Respondents

Husband Failure to Bring Paycheck Home Causes Marital Stress	Age of Respondents					
	Under 40		Over 40		Total	
	No.	%	No.	%	No.	%
Agree	123	92.5	63	98.4	186	94.4
Disagree	10	7.5	1	1.6	11	5.6
Total	133	67.5	64	32.5	197	100.0

Limitation on our earning potential and income is another reason that makes it imperative that our husbands bring their paycheck home. We thus determined whether Black husbands in Tidewater consistently bring their paycheck home. Our findings from Table 9 indicate that although a number of men desired their wives to help support their family, the use they sometimes made of their own paycheck became a problem. An overwhelming majority of the respondents (94 percent) agreed that it occurred when our husbands failed to bring all or the necessary amount of their paycheck home to support our households

Table 10

Consequences of Husbands' Failure to Bring Paycheck Home
by Age of Respondents

P a n e l	Reactions	Age of Respondents					
		Under 40		Over 40		Total	
		No.	%	No.	%	No.	%
A	Husband and Wife Argued	98	66.7	50	72.5	148	68.5
	Husband and Wife Did Not Argue	49	33.3	19	27.5	68	31.5
	Total	147	68.1	69	31.9	216	100.0
B	Husband and Wife Fought	61	41.5	32	46.4	93	43.1
	Husband and Wife Did Not Fight	86	58.5	37	53.6	123	56.9
	Total	147	68.1	69	31.9	216	100.0
C	Wife Borrowed Money to Pay Rent and Buy Food	64	43.5	31	44.9	95	44.0
	Wife Did Not Borrow Money to Pay Rent and Buy Food	83	56.5	38	55.1	121	56.0
	Total	147	68.1	69	31.9	216	100.0
D	Husband and Wife Separated	67	45.6	23	33.3	90	41.7
	Husband and Wife Did Not Separate	80	54.4	46	66.7	126	58.3
	Total	147	68.1	69	31.9	216	100.0

while only 6 percent of the respondents disagreed. When our husbands disappointed us, the household became a setting for varied types of stressful relations. Table 10 identifies such behavior by age of the Tidewater respondents. It indicates that the largest percentage of the respondents reported that it caused spouses to argue, but there were 73 percent of the women over forty as opposed to 67 percent under forty with this opinion. This question was pursued in greater detail among the twenty seven women in the follow up study. They reported that when Tidewater husbands did not bring their paycheck home, we argued with them about matters unrelated to bills as well as about unpaid debts. This finding indicates that some of the respondents considered economic support a primary factor in family life. As noted, by one respondent, "A man's love will not pay the rent and food bills." Not only did we argue about the failure of our spouses to bring all their paycheck home, but, as noted in Table 10, we also fought, 43 percent of the respondents said. However, a larger percentage of the respondents over forty (46 percent) than under forty (42 percent) agreed that fighting was a consequence of our husbands' failure to bring their paycheck home. Because a relatively small percentage of the respondents agreed that the problem led to fights than to arguments, perhaps this indicates that Black marriages were

73

not characteristically physically violent about the paycheck problem. As also shown in Table 10, another result of the paycheck problem was that we borrowed money to pay rent and buy food (44 percent). However, the most serious result for the family was spousal separation. Since only 42 percent of the respondents agreed that separation resulted from the paycheck problem, it was the least likely reaction.

These findings also indicate that the quality of our family life or whether it exists at all is connected with our husbands' use of their paychecks to support our households. Perhaps employers could alleviate this problem, to some extent, by establishing programs that educate Black male employees on the family dimension of their paycheck and, in turn, improved family relations may lead to higher job productivity.

Decision Making

An equally important type of behavior in Tidewater marriages is decision making. It was operationalized in the interviews as participation in the resolution of family problems. In reviewing the literature on decision making in the Black family, one finding stands out. The studies show that matrifocality, equalitarianism, and patriarchy are the authority patterns in the Black family. In general, each authority pattern has been identified with a particular social class, yet studies of modern Black family life have primarily focused on the low income and working class families. This review of the literature of decision making in Black marriages is begun with the matrifocal pattern. It is conceptualized as "close affective ties, domestic units dominated by females, and high frequencies of households" (Otterbein 1966:vii). The prevalence of a matriarchy, however, has been challenged by a number of writers. According to the Cromwells (1978:754-756), on the basis of their inner city neighborhood sample in Kansas City, and Staples (1977:174-183), using a historical perspective of family life, the concept of Black matriarchy must be rejected, for it is not the dominant relationship in the Black family.

However, there is some evidence of wife dominance in Black families, including the slave family. At the outset, it should be stated that the slave system helped regulate husband and wife relations. This means that some slave masters required couples to live together, respect their obligations to each other and refrain from adultery (Stampp 1963:341,42). On a Mississippi plantation, for example, when a wife failed to do the family cooking, washing and mending, the master at first admonished her, and when she did not adhere, he disci-

74

plined her with the whip (Stampp 1963:342). On the other hand, the slave system gave the wife more authority in the decision making process than was given the husband. Instead of being the head of the household, the husband served as an assistant, companion, and sex partner and was often considered as his wife's possession (Stampp 1963:344). Similarly, according to Frazier (1939:102-113), Hippler (1974:47), Moynihan (1967:30-31), and Powdermaker (1962:204), wife dominance is characteristic of modern Black low income families. In the Hunter's Point study by Hippler (1974:21), these households were described as headed either by a grandmother whose daughters and grandchildren lived with her or by a mother whose children lived with her. The female heads were the central figures and the only financial, emotional, and authority leaders in the household. In fact, the men were described as unsuited to steady employment (Hippler 1974:43,47). Likewise, the men in a Syracuse, New York low rent housing project experienced a high rate of unemployment (Willie 1976:137-138). The economic marginality of men in the settings, described by Hippler and Willie, tends to foster the maintenance of a Black matriarchy. Moreover, it has been found that Black matriarchy in the lower class is a consequence of slavery (Frazier 1939:102) and more recently of the economic insecurity of Afro-American males (Hippler 1974:217; Powdermaker 1962:205; Smith 1956:22; King 1945:103).

The literature of the Black family also indicates that there are several factors that prevent our men from being strong figures in our homes. They include segregated housing, poor schooling, and racial discrimination that function to undermine the morale of the Negro man and weaken his position in the family (Blood and Wolfe 1960:35). His position is also weakened because he has less education (Bernard 1966:90) and power in the home than his wife (Blood and Wolfe 1960: 34-35), and the Black man is often unemployed or earns a low wage (Moynihan 1967:65-71). Likewise, there is some evidence of wife dominance in the modern Black middle class family. For example, of the forty one households in Golden Towers, 16 were dominated by the wives (Barnes 1983:60); hence, the women made a majority of the decisions concerning their children, family activities, and social life (Barnes 1983:60-61).

Several studies have also examined patriarchal authority in the Black family. The studies vary on which groups manifest male dominance. For example, it was seen in Black working class communities in River-town County, Missouri and Pulpwood County, Florida (Martin and Martin 1978:20). Also, Scanzoni (1971:241) found that in the American

Black family, the higher the husband's occupational status, the more likely he will resolve conflict in his favor. Furthermore, Barnes (1983: 65-66) found that nine households in Golden Towers were husband dominated; "the men decided their schedules, approved the activities of their wives and children, and determined the use of household finances, but the women implemented a majority of their decisions and were responsible for the performance of household chores."

Many of the studies of decision making in Black families have also focused on the equalitarian pattern of authority. It was found to be the norm in working class marriages in an inner city neighborhood in Kansas City (Cromwell and Cromwell 1978:757) and in Rivertown and Pulpwood Counties (Martin and Martin 1978:20). It was also a feature of family life in Texas (Bullock 1941:29-30) and among middle-class spouses, "especially when both are employed" (Frazier, 1957:331). For example, in Golden Towers, sixteen of the couples had an equalitarian pattern of decision making (Barnes 1983:66). The couples manifested equal control over household decisions, but "there was a lot of give and take, and the best suggestions were accepted" (Barnes 1983:66). Similarly, Scanzoni (1971:241,242) noted that the occupational status of the husband in two thirds of Black American families determines who controls decision making. Scanzoni (1971:241,242) also noted that above the underclass in Indianapolis, there is no "overall wife dominance" pattern, which means that the Black male is "pressing for and has largely achieved equal authority with his wife," and "the tradition of female dominance appears to be expiring." Besides, Barnes (1983:61) found in Golden Towers that there is no pure decision making pattern; for example, she noted that "Although the women were leaders in the matriarchal households, the men were not completely outside the decision making process." Moreover, Barnes (1983:71) noted that in the patriarchal households, in Golden Towers, the men make only a majority of the family decisions, and sometimes in equalitarian households spouses make decisions independently of each other (Barnes 1983:66).

This literature of the decision making process in Black families indicates that varied types of authority patterns characterize Black marriages on all social class levels and that each marriage is comprised of all three authority patterns. The Tidewater respondents supported the view that female dominance is characteristic of Black marriages, but not to the exclusion of other patterns. The situation is that only wife dominance caused the Tidewater respondents concern. They seemed to believe that domination by one spouse hindered the effectual functioning of the home; that is, the ideas of each partner were needed

76

Table 11

Husbands Failed to Discuss Family Problems
by Age of respondents

Husbands Fail to Discuss Family Problems	Age of Respondents					
	Under 40		Over 40		Total	
	No.	%	No.	%	No.	%
Agree	102	72.3	38	53.5	140	66.0
Disagree	39	27.7	33	46.5	72	34.0
Total	141	66.5	71	33.5	212	100.0

Corrected Chi Square = 6.64143 with 1 degree of freedom
$P < 0.0100$

to arrive at the best solutions to problems. Hence, the respondents reported that women in Tidewater desired their husbands to take a more active role in household decision making. The data in Table 11 indicate that 66 percent of the respondents agreed that male spouses in Tidewater did not discuss family problems as much as desired. As also shown in Table 11, when age of the respondents was crosstabulated with this finding, more women under forty (72 percent) than over forty (54 percent) held this view. In all probability, this finding is a consequence of women under forty having more dependent children than women over forty, who required a relatively large number of decisions. Because the alpha value is .01, there is a significant relationship between age of respondents and their opinions that male spouses needed to enhance their role in the decision making process.

Next, we determined the consequences of husbands' failure to participate in the decision making process. Table 12 presents the results of this inquiry, however, the consequences of husbands' failure to participate in the decision making process and the age of the respondents were not found statistically significant, spousal separation excepted. Although the remainder of Table 12 is not statistically significant, it is informative. For example, the most frequent reaction to the low level of husband participation in the decision making process was decision making and telling our spouses later (61 percent) or

Table 12

Consequences of Husbands' Failure to Adequately Engage In The Decision
Making Process by Age of Respondents

P a n e l	Consequences	Under 40 No.	Under 40 %	Over 40 No.	Over 40 %	Total No.	Total %
		Age of Respondents					
A	Wives Implement Decisions And Inform Spouses	92	62.6	41	58.6	133	61.3
	Wives Did Not Implement Decisions And Inform Spouses	55	37.4	29	41.4	84	38.7
	Total	147	67.7	70	32.3	217	100.0
B	Wives Made Decisions Unbeknowing to Spouse	93	63.3	37	52.9	130	59.9
	Wives Did Not Make Decisions Unbeknowing to Spouse	54	36.7	33	47.1	87	40.1
	Total	147	67.7	70	32.3	217	100.0
C	Husbands And Wives Argued	77	52.4	37	52.9	114	52.5
	Husbands And Wives Did Not Argue	70	47.6	33	47.1	103	47.5
	Total	147	67.7	70	32.3	217	100.0
D	Wives Held Responsible For House- Hold Problems	59	41.8	25	35.2	84	39.6
	Wives Were Not Held Responsible For Household Problems	82	58.2	46	64.8	128	60.4
	Total	141	66.5	71	33.5	212	100.0
E	Spouses Separate	53	36.1	15	21.4	68	31.3
	Spouses Did Not Separate	94	63.9	55	78.6	149	68.7
	Total	147	67.7	70	32.3	217	100.0

Panel E:
Corrected Chi Square = 4.05911 with 1 degree of freedom
$P < 0.0439$

making decisions unbeknowing to our spouses (60 percent). We also
argued with our spouses about their low participation in the decision
making process. Of course, the most interesting finding in Table
12 is that, although some Tidewater husbands failed to help manage
their household, they blamed their wife for family problems (40
percent).

Even though this point is interesting, perhaps the most serious result
of husbands' failure to participate in the decision making process
is spousal separation in Table 12. However, the largest percentage
of the respondents, especially older women (79 percent), did not hold
this view. Of the respondents, with this opinion, 36 percent was under
forty while 21 percent was over forty. The alpha value (.04) indicates

that a significant relationship exists between age of respondents and the view that husbands' failure to participate in the decision making process led to separation.

Husbands' Household Repair Skills

Not only did husband failure to help manage the household lead to stress, but their lack of mechanical knowledge also caused problems. According to Tidewater respondents, we wanted our husbands to make household repairs; the distribution of the responses to this question is presented in Table 13. Of course, some two-thirds of the sample stated that Black women did not experience stress as a result of such husband behavior, and a larger percentage of the women over forty than under forty held this view. As expected, of the third of the respondents who believed that we experienced problems with our husbands when they could not make household repairs, younger women, more often than older women, held this opinion. Because the alpha value is .02, a significant relationship obtains between the two variables.

Table 13

Husbands' Lack of Household Repair Knowledge
caused Marital Stress by Age of Respondents

Husbands' Lack of Household Repair Knowledge Causes Stress	Age of Respondents					
	Under 40		Over 40		Total	
	No.	%	No.	%	No.	%
Agree	55	39.0	16	22.5	71	33.5
Disagree	86	61.0	55	77.5	141	66.5
Total	141	66.5	71	33.5	212	100.0

Corrected Chi Square = 5.03631 with 1 degree of freedom
$P < 0.0248$

Husband-Wife Emotional Relations

The emotional bond was another concern in the marriages of Black women in Tidewater. The affective relations in Black marriages have always concerned social researchers. Starting with the Black family, during slavery, there were a number of factors that influenced affective relations between spouses. For instance, the limited rule of the father, absence of legal marriages, the family's limited social and economic means, and separations at auctions resulted in unstable families (Stampp 1963:344). The consequences of instability were reflected in the husband and wife bond. Some couples lacked "deep and endearing affection," and the couples who were separated at auctions found it easy to take new spouses in their new homes (Stampp 1963:345). On the other hand, it appears that affection characterized some marital relations. For example, Gutman 1976:153) has noted that the true extent of husband and wife affection was related to the length of marriage. Thus, couples who had been married a long time experienced more suffering as a result of forced separations than marriages of shorter duration. Although Frazier (1957:125,229) did not discuss the emotional bond in the Black bourgeoisie marriages, he seems to indicate that the segment of this class that resided in Durham and the intellectuals were family oriented. Hence, there may have been a relatively strong emotional bond between the spouses. On the other hand, the emotional bond between Black women and men is clearer in the low income family. It has been indicated that the man's economic position and the competition between women to obtain affectional and sexual satisfaction weaken their bond (Drake and Cayton 1945:583). This competition tempts men "to trade love for a living," which develops an attitude of suspicion "toward men blended with a woman's natural desire to be loved for herself alone" (Drake and Cayton 1945:584). Although Black spouses desire companionship, physical affection, and empathy from marriage, it is difficult to achieve (see Chapter 1).

On the basis of these findings, we determined whether a strong emotional bond characterized Black marriages in Tidewater. It was operationalized in the interviews as husband warmth, tenderness, and loving care that involved verbalization of love for wives, touching, and kissing. According to the data in Table 14, 57 percent of the respondents stated that our husbands did not display these emotional qualities to us, but a larger percentage of the women over than under forty held this opinion. When we found that our spouses in Tidewater were unkind to us, we reacted varied ways. Table 15 presents two types of reactions that we manifested. The most frequent type of reaction

Table 14

Tidewater Husbands Failed to Show Wives Love, Warmth, and Affection by Age of Respondents

Husbands Fail to Show Wives Love, Warmth, and Affection	Age of Respondents					
	Under 40		Over 40		Total	
	No.	%	No.	%	No.	%
Agree	76	53.9	45	63.4	121	57.1
Disagree	65	46.1	26	36.6	91	42.9
Total	141	66.5	71	33.5	212	100.0

was tension, operationalized in the interviews as stress. There is not much difference between the respondents under forty (97 percent) and the respondents over forty (96 percent) with this opinion. The next most frequent type of reaction was for us to feel insecure and unloved, however, in this case, a larger percentage of the women over forty (97 percent) than under forty (92 percent) reported that we feel this way.

Table 15

Results of Unkind Wife Treatment by Age of Respondents

Panel	Reactions by Wives to Unkind Treatment by Husbands	Age of Respondents					
		Under 40		Over 40		Total	
		No.	%	No.	%	No.	%
A	Feel Tension	137	96.5	64	95.5	201	96.2
	Do Not Feel Tension	5	3.5	3	4.5	8	3.8
	Total	142	67.9	67	32.1	209	100.0
B	Feel Insecure and Unloved	124	91.9	59	96.7	183	93.4
	Do Not Feel Unsecure and Unloved	11	8.1	2	3.3	13	6.6
	Total	135	68.9	61	31.1	196	100.0

81

Table 16

Husbands' Unfaithfulness
By Age of Respondents

| Husbands are Unfaithful | Age of Respondents | | | | | |
| | Under 40 | | Over 40 | | Total | |
	No.	%	No.	%	No.	%
Agree	99	70.2	45	63.4	144	67.9
Disagree	42	29.8	26	36.6	68	32.1
Total	141	66.5	71	33.5	212	100.0

Husband infidelity was the second type of unkind behavior that the respondents identified in our Tidewater marriages. As seen in Table 16, a large percentage (68 percent) of the respondents agreed that our Tidewater husbands were unfaithful, but a larger percentage of the women under forty (70 percent) than over forty (63 percent) held this opinion. In the follow up study, comprised of twenty seven respondents, we asked the women to describe marriage infidelity. One respondent described several types of marriage unfaithfulness, including the trio arrangement. This was a practice whereby a man, single or married, dated simultaneously two women who were friends or women he brought together. While with them, he sat or walked between them and kissed and engaged in sex with each. There was also another type of group arrangement that included three, five, or seven people. An even number of males and females, with the exception of the odd person, who may be either sex, made up this group. Because this relationship did not require much time and money, a husband could easily be unfaithful. Though these alternate sexual arrangements were diversions for some husbands, they were not the main trouble makers. Instead, it was the infidelity that occurred when a husband built an economic and/or sexual relationship with another woman that caused problem marriages. According to Liebow (1967:123), in TALLY'S CORNER, extramarital behavior may damage relations between spouses.

Of course, it appears that we reacted various ways when our husbands were unfaithful. As indicated in Table 17, one of our primary reactions, in the opinion of the respondents, was jealousy and suspicion of other women (47 percent). Unlike the insecurity and unloved variables, it was found that a larger percentage of the younger (51 percent) than older women (39 percent) held this opinion. Further, the respondents indicated that husband unfaithfulness led to varied types of jealousy, including limitations on our husbands' dance behavior. As illustrated in Table 17, a larger percentage of the respondents under forty (28 percent) than over forty (17 percent) agreed that we limit our husbands' dancing. According to the respondents, in the follow up study, some of us only allowed our spouse to dance once or twice with another woman. Though some husbands deviated with penalty, they were indeed forbidden to dance with other women on slow music. In either case, we reacted by leaving the dance, changing our facial expression, cutting in on their dance, getting angry, and telling our husbands, "You are dancing too much with that woman." On the other hand, some of us handled husband dancing with other women by dancing two or three times with another man. When this happened, one respondent says, her husband became angry and paid her more attention.

There were also some respondents whose husbands danced a great deal with other women, yet they did not get angry. For example, one respondent stated, "My husband dances a lot with other women, but it does not bother me, so long as he comes back often and asks me to dance." This respondent had noticed two things about married couples who danced only with each other. They were insecure and, as she put it, she "knew more dirt on them, husbands and wives, than she knew about other couples."

On the other hand, some respondents' husbands danced with them all evening. One of them reported her situation thusly: "That Turkey (my husband) dances with me all evening and refuses to dance with other women. What happens is that he baby sits me at dances, and it makes me mad, for I want to laugh and talk with other people."

Another indication of wife jealousy and suspicion of other women was that we disliked our husbands looking into the eyes of other women. That is, we did not give our husbands an opportunity to have sustained eye contact and conversation with other women. As seen in Table 17, 35 percent of the respondents under forty and 36 percent of the respondents over forty held this view. We did not want our husbands looking, for sustained periods, at other women, because of its effects on us. The women in the follow up study explained how we felt by

Table 17

Results of Husband Infidelity by Age of Respondents

P a n e l	Reactions by Wives to Husbands' Infidelity	Age of Respondents					
		Under 40		Over 40		Total	
		No.	%	No.	%	No.	%
A	Jealous and Suspicious of Other Women	74	51.0	27	38.6	101	47.0
	Not Jealous and Suspicious of Other Women	71	49.0	43	61.4	114	53.0
	Total	145	67.4	70	32.6	215	100.0
B	Limit Husband's Dance Behavior With Other Women	41	28.3	12	17.1	53	24.7
	Do Not Limit Husband's Dance Behavior With Other Women	104	71.7	58	82.9	162	75.3
	Total	145	67.4	70	32.6	215	100.0
C	Restrict Husband's Eye Contact With Other Women	51	35.2	25	35.7	76	35.3
	Do Not Restrict Husband's Eye Contact With Other Women	94	64.8	45	64.3	139	64.7
	Total	145	67.4	70	32.6	215	100.0
D	Limit Time Husbands Hold Women Hands During Introduction	41	28.3	14	20.0	55	25.6
	Do Not Limit Time Husbands Hold Women Hands During Introduction	104	71.7	56	80.0	160	74.4
	Total	145	67.4	70	32.6	215	100.0
E	Argue With Husbands	104	71.7	45	64.3	149	69.3
	Do Not Argue With Husbands	41	28.3	25	35.7	66	30.7
	Total	145	67.4	70	32.6	215	100.0
F	Fight With Husbands	82	56.6	31	44.3	113	52.6
	Do Not Fight With Husbands	63	43.4	39	55.7	102	47.4
	Total	145	67.4	70	32.6	215	100.0
G	Refuse to Converse With Husbands	87	60.0	33	47.1	120	55.8
	Do Not Refuse to Converse With Husbands	58	40.0	37	52.9	95	44.2
	Total	145	67.4	70	32.6	215	100.0
H	Retire to Different Sleeping Quarters	73	50.8	38	55.1	111	51.9
	Do Not Retire to Different Sleeping Quarters	72	49.7	31	44.9	103	48.1
	Total	145	67.8	69	32.2	214	100.0
I	Take a Lover	110	90.2	49	79.0	159	86.4
	Do Not Take a Lover	12	9.8	13	21.0	25	13.6
	Total	122	66.3	62	33.7	184	100.0

Panel I:
  Corrected Chi Square = 3.44232 with 1 degree of freedom
  $P < 0.0373$

relating their feelings when their husbands "gazed," "stared," or looked into the eyes of other women. It belittled them, made them feel bad, and wonder what other women had that they did not have. However, it was probably not that other women had more going for themselves than wives; instead, it is likely that the tension resulting in spousal relations limited our emotional bonding in marriage. Of course, all of us did not respond this way to our husbands' eye contact with other women. For example, when the husband of one respondent looked at another woman, she looked at another man. In still another case, a respondent reported that while her husband was looking into the eyes of another woman, some man was looking into her eyes, a type of behavior that caused her husband to soon ask, "Who is that man looking at you?" On the other hand, some women were more direct about their dislike for such behavior. For example, one respondent related, "I have gotten jealous when my husband looked at another woman, and I said a few choice words, but that stopped him only for the moment. He carried me home and went back out and looked at somebody else; thus, if anybody goes lacking, it is the woman." In another case, a respondent stated, "When my husband looks into the eyes of another woman, I mention it to him and ask why he is looking so hard. It is not the looking that counts, but it is the lustful look in his eyes." When other respondents saw their husbands gazing into the eyes of other women, they became sarcastic, cold, snobbish, or angry. Of course, one attractive professional wife only got jealous of husband gazing when the woman looked as good or better than she did, for she thinks, "that his taste in women must be as good as what he has."

According to the respondents, husband infidelity led to a multiplicity of other types of behavior, including regulation of time our spouses held women's hands during introductions, arguments, fights, temporary silence, and retreat to different sleeping quarters. Moreover, the respondents stated that some of us took lovers when we found our husbands unfaithful. Of the 86 percent of the sample who agreed that husband infidelity led to wife infidelity, a larger percentage of the women under forty (90 percent) than over forty (79 percent) held this opinion. We next asked the respondents why some of us took lovers when we found our husbands unfaithful. They stated that it happened because we had unfulfilled needs, such as a positive self image that comes from admiration; that is, in the opinion of the respondents, when our appearance and work, housekeeping, and cooking skills are not admired and complimented, and when we do not feel cared for, we do not feel good about ourselves. It would seem, from the respondents' comments that when we have a low self image, it is evident in our appearance, attitude, and facial glow, and that we desire enhancement in all areas. When our needs were not fulfilled, some of us turned to extramarital affairs to save our marriage, obtain sex, money, and happiness. For example, the young attractive business woman, whom we mentioned earlier, stated, "I like .to laugh and, therefore, I go out to lunch with male friends and enjoy conversation and laughter over drinks and food, enjoyment that I do not get from my husband." It seems clear that the respondents believed that we did not want to be in a position to need a male friend; nevertheless, some of us found ourselves in such situation. In fact, the respondents often stated that they were a one man woman; however, they noted that, unfortunately, they needed more than one man. For example, a divorcee stated that she did not feel that one man could provide all the things a woman needs. In her case, she had developed friendship with three supportive males whom she enjoyed; moreover, they were men in whom she confided and who collectively gave her a well-rounded experience. This finding seems to indicate that the male child-rearing process needs to be strengthened to the extent that our men are more well rounded. The divorcee also stated that, although "Some single women fall in love with married men, a woman must stay in control of the situation -- otherwise, it will be a disastrous experience."

The respondents were asked what, indeed, does happen in extramarital relations? They noted that our lovers sometimes cause marital separation while some of us boast about our extramarital experiences. Further, a respondent says that we soon face, in our new relationships, many of the same problems encountered with our husbands. It would thus seem that some of us fall back into a rut and end up in a worse position than before we took a lover. It, therefore, appears that when we tried to escape the frustration and worry involved in husband infidelity, we ended up experiencing problems away from home as well as at home. However, according to the divorcee, discussed earlier, this is a problem that we bring upon ourselves. This respondent believes that female networks are one answer to our problem; that is, we, as Black women, in her opinion, need to stop directing all our energy to our men and utilize some of it in other satisfying outlets. She stated it this way:

We nag, criticize, and condemn our spouses, because we have neither established relationships with other Black women to the extent that we can confide in them and provide mutual support, nor have we gotten to the point that we have alternatives. This means that the Black man is every thing to some of us and resentment builds up, because our sexual needs are not met. Black women are responsible for problems between the sexes, for they have the opportunity to make their sons the kind of men they want them to be. Some women take it for granted that it is the mans' role to teach their sons how to treat women. But this should not be the case, because they do not have such knowledge. I have two sons, and I am teaching them how to deal gently with Black womanhood. Black women do well, but they must get into themselves and define themselves. I choose factors that work for me; that is, I need people in my life whom I can use, but not misuse. In my relations with others, I must offer them something, and, in turn, I must get something. This is the way I am in the workplace and elsewhere. My girlfriends and I, for example, have a friendship network that provides baby sitting help, hot meals, and a number of other services.

It appears that the respondent is arguing that we invest too much in our men and not enough in ourselves and our women. It would also seem that the respondent has summed up our relationship with men, because, indeed, we expend a lot of energy keeping our husbands in check and serving as co-breadwinner or the primary breadwinner in our homes. If we diverted our energy, in a wholesome and satisfying way, to other male and female friends, husband infidelity may prove not only less consequential, but it may cause our husbands to be kinder to us.

Interestingly, the stress developed from worry and frustration that results from husbands' extramarital life does not end at home, but it also affects our relations in the community. That is, we are more likely to vent our frustrations on other women than would occur, if less stress characterized our marriages. Because Black couples share the common burden of race, because, as this chapter and Chapter 2 have shown, we share a common economic struggle, it should be easy to improve our marriage relations and, thereby, improve our relations with other women.

REFERENCES CITED

Barnes, Annie S.
1971   THE BLACK FAMILY IN GOLDEN TOWERS. Charlottesville: University of Virginia. Doctoral Dissertation.

Barnes, Annie S.
1977   "The Economic and Social Structure of the Atlanta Community." JOURNAL OF SOCIAL BEHAVIOR

238:353-360

Barnes, Annie S.
1983   "Black Husbands and Wives: An Assessment of Marital Roles in A Middle-Class Neighborhood." In Constance E. Obudho (ed.) BLACK MARRIAGE AND FAMILY THERAPY. Westport: Greenwood Press.

Bernard, Jessie
1966   MARRIAGE AND FAMILY AMONG NEGROES. Englewood Cliffs: Prentice-Hall, Inc.

Billingsley, Andrew T.
1968   BLACK FAMILIES IN WHITE AMERICA. Englewood Cliffs: Prentice-Hall, Inc.

Blood, Robert O. and Donald M. Wolfe
1960   HUSBANDS AND WIVES. New York: Free Press

Brimmer, Andrew
1978   "Economic Perspectives." BLACK ENTERPRISE 9:57

Brimmer, Andrew
1978   "Economic Perspectives." BLACK ENTERPRISE 9:120

Bullock, Henry Allen
1941   THE TEXAS NEGRO FAMILY: THE STATUS OF ITS
        SOCIO-ECONOMIC ORGANIZATION. Prairie View: Prairie
        View College Press.

Cromwell, Vickey L. and Ronald E. Cromwell
1978   "Perceived Dominance in Decision-Making and Conflict
        Resolution among Anglo, Black and Chicano Couples."
        JOURNAL OF MARRIAGE AND THE FAMILY. 40:749-759.

Drake St. Clair and Horace R. Clayton
1945   BLACK METROPOLIS, II. New York: Harper and Row
        Publishers.

Frazier, Franklin
1932   THE FREE NEGRO FAMILY. Nashville: Fisk University
        Press.

Frazier, E. Franklin
1939   THE NEGRO FAMILY IN THE UNITED STATES. Chicago:
        The University of Chicago Press.

Frazier, E. Franklin
1957   THE BLACK BOURGEOISIE. New York: Free Press.

Gutman, Herbert G.
1976   THE BLACK FAMILY IN SLAVERY AND FREEDOM, 1750-
        1925. New York: Pantheon Press.

Hawkins, Homer
1976   "Urban Housing and the Black Family." PHYLON 37:73-84.

Hippler, Arthur E.
1974   HUNTER'S POINT. New York: Basic Books, Inc.

Holloman, Regina E. and Fannie E. Lewis
1978   "The Clan: Case Study of a Black Extended Family in Chica-
        go." In Demitri B. Shimkin et al. (eds.) THE EXTENDED
        FAMILY IN BLACK SOCIETIES. The Hague: Mouton Pub-
        lisher, pp. 201-238.

King, Charles E.
1945   "The Negro Maternal Family: A Product of An Economic and A Culture System." SOCIAL FORCES 24:100-104.

Kunkel, Peter and Sara Sue Kennard
1971   SPOUT SPRING. New York: Holt, Rinehart and Winston, Inc.

Liebow, Elliot
1967   TALLY'S CORNER. Boston: Little, Brown and Co.

Martin, Elmer P. and Joanne Mitchell Martin
1978   THE BLACK EXTENDED FAMILY. Chicago: The University of Chicago Press.

Miller, Herman
1964   RICH MAN, POOR MAN. New York: Thomas Y. Crowell

Moynihan, Daniel P.
1967   "The Roots of the Problem." In Lee Rainwater and William L. Yancey (eds.) THE MOYNIHAN REPORT AND THE POLITICS OF CONTROVERSY. Cambridge: The M. I. T. Press.

Nelson, Charmeynne D.
1975   "Myths About Black Women Workers in America." THE BLACK SCHOLAR, pp. 11-15.

Otterbein, Keith F.
1966   THE ANDROS ISLANDERS. Lawrence: University of Kansas Publishers.

Powdermaker, Hortense
1962   COPPER TOWN: CHANGING AFRICA. New York: Harper & Row Publishers.

Rodgers-Rose, La Frances
1980   THE BLACK WOMAN. Beverly Hills: Sage Publishers.

Russell, John
1913   THE FREE NEGRO IN VIRGINIA. Baltimore: Johns Hopkins Press.

Scanzoni, John H.
1971 THE BLACK FAMILY IN MODERN SOCIETY. Boston: Allyn & Bacon

Shimkin, Demitri B.
1978 "The Black Extended Family: A Basic Rural Institution and A Mechanism of Urban Adaptation." In Demitri B. Shimkin et al. (eds.) THE EXTENDED FAMILY IN BLACK SOCIETIES. The Hague. Mouton Publishers.

Smith, Raymond T.
1956 THE NEGRO FAMILY IN BRITISH GUIANA. New York: Grove Press.

Stampp. Kenneth M.
1963 THE PECULIAR INSTITUTION. New York: Alfred A. Knopf

Staples, Robert
1977 "The Myth of The Black Matriarchy." In Doris Y. Wilkinson and Ronald L. Taylor (eds.) THE BLACK MALE IN AMERICA. Chicago: Nelson Hall Publishers.

Starobin, Robert S.
1970 INDUSTRIAL SLAVERY IN THE OLD SOUTH. New York: Oxford University Press.

U.S. Department of Labor
1968-69 THE ATLANTA URBAN EMPLOYMENT SURVEY. Atlanta: Southeastern Regional Office, p. 14.

Willie, Charles V.
1970 THE FAMILY LIFE OF BLACK PEOPLE. Columbus: Charles E. Merrill

Willie, Charles V.
1976 A NEW LOOK AT BLACK FAMILIES. Bayside: General Hall, Inc.

CHAPTER FOUR

THE BLACK WOMAN IN THE COMMUNITY

Introduction

After work, the Tidewater respondents devote time to their spouses and management of their household considered in Chapter 3. We expect our husbands to work and bring their paycheck home, help with household decision making, make household repairs, and enhance our marital bond. What remains is a limited amount of time for community activities. We participate in religious, civic, and social organizations with women from varied neighborhoods in our city (Barnes 1979:132-137), as well as nearby cities. Barnes (1979:129,138) found in a study of voluntary associations in Atlanta that "social organizations focus on recreation while worship is the main emphasis in the church. However, according to Barnes (1979:129), "the identification of groups as social or religious merely denotes their primary goals and not their total perspective; hence, social groups participate in church-related activities while the churches sometimes sponsor social affairs."

The origin of voluntary association participation among Blacks is in the church and goes back to slavery. At that time, there were slave owners who required Blacks to attend their services while some owners permitted Black preachers to conduct church meetings, and a few slaves held secret church meetings in their homes. The church "is the only social institution of Negroes which started in the African forest and survived slavery" (Dubois 1898:6). The oppression and limited opportunities of the slavery era enhanced its significance (Frazier 1957:14) among Blacks. Even today, the church is still "the most pervasive community organization in six Negro communities in Tampa, Florida" (Ross and Wheeler 1971:203). Moreover, according to a national survey, 83 percent of the Black population attends church at least once a month and nearly half attend church at least twice a month (Brink and Harris 1964:220-221). For example, Barnes (1979:130) found, in "Golden Towers, a Black middle class neighborhood in northwest Atlanta, that the residents have attended Sunday School and church since childhood, but only a few families now attend Sunday School. However, in eighteen of the forty-one households, all the children and/or husbands and wives attend church, and in the remainder of the households at least one person goes to church on Sunday morning, but the women attend church more regularly than the men."

Although a few Black Americans attend white churches, Drake and Cayton (1945:413) found that only 10 percent of Negro church-goers in Chicago attend interracial churches and that in the South there is even less race mixing in the church. For example, "Atlanta is a southern group that holds membership mainly in Black churches, however, they are not distributed evenly among the denominations. For example, three-fourths of the Golden Towers women are Protestant and belong to several denominations, but the majority are Baptist and Methodist" (Barnes 1979:130).

This review of the literature indicates that Black women's participation in voluntary organizations goes back to church groups. With this beginning, middle class Black women now participate in social and civic organizations, such as Jack and Jill of America, that are strongly oriented toward activities that benefit all children. Nevertheless, there is variation in voluntary association participation; for example, in the Atlanta Black subsociety, all Blacks "do not have equal access to the adaptive functions of social organizations." Consequently, the middle class participates in social, civic, and religious groups while the working and lower classes make more use of the church as a means of self expression (Barnes 1979:139). Willie (1976:161) has also noted, in two case studies of poor families in the Cardoza section of Washington, D.C., that "The number of families with members participating in neighborhood associations is miniscule."

After determining that Black women engage in religious, social, and civic activities, the next inquiry focused on the interpersonal relations among women in community groups. Although several studies focus on Black women, including THE BLACK WOMAN IN AMERICA by Robert Staples, "TOGETHER" BLACK WOMEN by Inez Smith Reid, and TOMORROW'S TOMORROW by Joyce Ladner, neither is about the interpersonal relations between Black women. Instead, the study by Staples (1973:4) is about the "sexual oppression of Black women"; thus it focuses on the general life of Black women, marriage, motherhood, and the woman's liberation movement. Similarly, Reid's (1972:10) study deals with militancy as a viable solution to Black oppression" while Ladner's (1972:14) study of teenage girls in TOMORROW'S

93

TOMORROW focused on "(1) life histories and (2) attitudes and behavior that reflected approaching womanhood." Although each of these studies is vital to understanding the texture of the Black experience, only minimal attention is given to interpersonal relations of Black women.

However, there are at least two exceptions to this literature, including THE BLACK WOMAN by LaFrances Rodgers-Rose. This volume is concerned with "how Black women handle various problems that confront them," their "values," support mechanisms of the extended family," "relationships between Black men and women," attitudes of Black women "toward the women's liberation movement," and the "roles of Black women in the family" (Rodgers-Rose 1980:12). It goes beyond the Black woman and family life and focuses on interpersonal relations between Black men and women and Black women and the feminist movement. Hence, this book "presents new ways of looking at not only the everyday life of Black women, but also the everyday life of Black people, including Black men and Black children" (Rodgers-Rose 1980-12). The next exception is BLACK MARRIAGE AND FAMILY THERAPY, by Constance E. Obudho. This book also goes beneath the surface of family relationships and tells us something about the feelings of marriage partners. It thus focuses on the "expression of love among Black people, husband-wife relationships, women's feelings about working and being wives and mothers, and some of the styles and processes of parenthood as well as family planning" along with "Marital and Family Therapy" (Obudho 1983:xiii). The Obudho and Rodgers-Rose books probe more deeply the interpersonal relations, especially between marriage partners, than any other works. In effect, they have laid the groundwork that challenges social scientists to begin looking at the essence of Black female relationships. This chapter takes up the challenge by describing Black women's attitudes toward the women's liberation movement as well as toward other Black women. Admitedly, this is not an easy task, for as Rodgers-Rose has pointed out, sociologists "have studied the outward status characteristics of income, education, occupation, and sexual compatibility" in the lives of Black women rather than probing beneath social behavior (see Chapter 1).

However, we found a small literature about varied types of behavior, including kin relations, among Black women. The family literature indicates that these relationships are not only consistent, but that there is a great deal of behavior among kinswomen, including communication. As Barnes (1981:360) has noted, the black women in Golden Towers, a middle class neighborhood in Atlanta, communicate with their kinsmen by writing letters, telephoning, and visiting while McAdoo (1979:79) has noted that Black family members in the working and middle class in Columbia, Maryland and Washington, D.C. see each other often, and Jack (1978:234-269) found that there appears to be a good deal of visiting in an extended family in New Orleans. Kinswomen also communicate with each other at family reunions. On such festive occasions, middle class kinsmen serve food jointly and engage in lively conversation (Barnes 1981:370-372). Similarly, kinsmen in Holmes County, Mississippi also serve food and greet one another at extended family gatherings (Shimkin 1978:66).

Black kinswomen also help each other a number of other ways, including financial assistance. As an example, eighteen of the forty one middle class families in Golden Towers had given their families such financial help as payment of property taxes, college fees, and food and furniture bills (Barnes 1983:372). According to Barnes (1983:372), "It was given on the husband and wife side to nieces, aunts, nephews, brothers, sisters, uncles, parents, and married children and their families." Likewise, working and middle class kinsmen in Columbia, Maryland and Washington, D.C. traded financial help, advice, and services (McAdoo 1979:33). A similar pattern was found in several other communities. The working class kinsmen in Pulpwood County, Florida, Newton County, Missouri, Cleveland, and Kansas City gave their kinsmen financial support (Martin and Martin 1978:29-31) while relatives in Holmes County, Mississippi gave each other shelter, food, and clothing in emergencies (Jack 1978:260), and lower income kinsmen in Jackson Harbor, a midwestern community, exchanged resources, possessions, and services (Stack 1975:33). These findings indicate that regardless of income level, helping patterns are part of the fabric of life in Black extended families.

Black kinswomen also give each other help with child care. In Golden Towers, for example, "over half the households had received help in rearing their children (Barnes 1981:372). Also, in Columbia, Maryland and Washington, D.C., "weekend child care was exchanged most commonly by an average of 35 percent of the families. Most of them used day-care or after-school programs to take care of their children during the week (McAdoo 1979:79). It has also been noted that in Holmes County, Mississippi "Children are readily transferred from the care of an unmarried mother or immature parent, say, to that of grandparents or an uncle or aunt" (Shimkin 1978:72). On the other hand, among the poor in the midwestern city of Jackson Harbor, child keeping is not only a usual pattern among kinsmen, but it also enables parents "to cope with poverty" (Stack 1974:62). Kinswomen of both

95

spouses help with child care. For example, the kinswomen of the Golden Towers residents who assist them with child care include paternal and maternal parents, sisters, and aunts and nieces" (Barnes 1981:373). Further, "Yvonne Flowers has pointed out that the residence of an aunt was often a welcome home for different members of the family" (Lorde 1979:52).

The kinswomen also provide mutual emotional support. For instance, Martin and Martin (1978:2,31) noted in their study of residents in "two small-town areas in Central Missouri and northern Florida and two urban areas, Cleveland and Kansas City," that, "For some people, the extended family provided moral support in troubled times, such as a difficult divorce or separation." There is also closeness among kinswomen in everyday matters. As seen in Golden Towers, wives considered their closest friends to include their sisters, mothers, brothers, cousins, aunts, and nieces (Barnes 1981:373). Another finding is that there is a closer relationship between adult female siblings and between them and their male siblings than between male siblings" (Barnes 1981:373).

These findings in the family literature indicate that Black kinswomen on the middle, working, and low income levels depend upon each other. They share resouces, services, and emotional support.

We next determined the nature of interpersonal relations in helping patterns. Stack (1970:36) found in Jackson Harbor that "Close kin who have relied upon one another over the years often complain about the sacrifices they have made and the deprivation they have endured for one another." Similarly, it was found in Golden Towers that the financial helping pattern leads to some family stress, however, according to one respondent, if relatives seemed appreciative, it would be less difficult (Barnes 1981:372). On the other hand, among middle class and working families in Columbia, Maryland and Washington, D.C., McAdoo (1979:110) noted that "most of the parents said that they were not operating out of a burdensome sense of obligation, but were simply acting because, as they often put it, "this is what is done in families." However, "Overall, 16 percent said that they felt a little pressure to share from their families; 21 percent said "some," and only 8 percent said a great deal." Not only does the literature indicate that financial help is a usual pattern in Black families, but it also suggests that it sometimes causes stress. The result of this analysis is that it provides some insight into interpersonal relations between relatives in helping patterns.

The unity among non-kinswomen is not as well known. Nevertheless, a search of the literature of Black women indicates that nonkinswomen have also worked to achieve common goals, including liberation of our race. For example, as soon as Sojourner Truth was liberated, by the State of New York in 1817, she joined the Abolition movement and delivered anti-slavery lectures (Brown 1971:13-14). Like Sojourner Truth, Harriet Tubman, a somewhat younger woman, who escaped from a Maryland plantation, participated in the abolition movement and led some 400 slaves to freedom (Brown 1971:57). Besides working together for liberation of the race, Black women have also worked together for liberation of their own sex; for example, Sojourner Truth and Maria Stewart worked to achieve rights for Black women. Stewart, an ardent spokeswoman, scorned the inconsistent views of femininity which allowed Black women to experience the drudgery of domestic work but not entry into public life and insisted that only individual capacities should set the boundaries of individual growth (Lowenberg and Bogin 1976:25). Moreover, Stewart compared the plight of Black women with that of white women by noting that they were denied employment in the "comparatively restricted areas open to white women" (Lowenberg and Bogin 1976:29). Working for the same cause, Sojourner Truth campaigned for the rights of Black women in the context of the feminist movement. It appears that Sojourner Truth was the only Black woman who consistently identified with the nineteenth century feminist movement as well as the only Black woman present at the First National Woman's Rights Convention in Worcester, Massachusetts in 1850 (Lerner 1972:568). A resolution was passed at that convention bemoaning the servitude of Black women and promising their effort to obtain their rights (Lerner 1972:568). In 1851, Sojourner Truth participated in another women's convention in Akron, Ohio, but a dozen or so of the feminists asked Frances D. Gage, the presiding officer, to prevent her from speaking, for they felt that the feminists' cause would get mixed up with abolition. Nevertheless, it was Sojourner Truth's speech that brought order to the somewhat stormy convention (Lowenberg and Bogin 1976:245,252). Some sixteen years later, Sojourner Truth attended the Convention of the American Equal Rights Association in New York City. Even though women's rights and abolition had been closely linked for about twenty years, a rift occurred at this convention, because Negro men were not willing to link their suffrage with female suffrage (Downs 1943:30). Thus, they spoke for themselves, white women spoke for themselves, and only "Sojourner Truth spoke for those doubly opposed by race and sex" (Rollins 1964:35-36). According to these findings, Sojourner Truth and Stewart were unified in their common endeavor to achieve the rights of Black women, and Sojourner Truth and Harriett Tubman worked to achieve liberation of our race.

97

Tidewater Black Women and the Women's Liberation Movement

Because Sojourner Truth attempted in the nineteenth century feminist movement to obtain the rights of Black women, the Tidewater respondents were asked whether the feminist movement in the twentieth century is the panacea for Black women's problems. According to 114 of the respondents, it was not the answer to our problems. This finding has been supported by Slaby and Sealy (1973:197) who noted that "The question of liberation of women somehow does not appear to be relevant to Black women or, if it is relevant, seems of less importance than the liberation as blacks." The respondents were also asked why the feminist movement was not the solution to our problems. Their responses were varied, and support the finding by Slaby and Sealy. Thus, the Tidewater respondents reported that we had liberation needs that differed from the liberation needs of white women; for example, a civil service employee in her twenties, noted:

Personally, I don't think that we belong in the feminist movement because, as long as we have been in this country, we have been liberated from the home and sometimes forced to work as hard as our men. As a result, we do not need the type of liberation white women are seeking. Nevertheless, we need other types of liberation, such as liberation from our men. They have just begun to treat us like ladies, for they have only recently obtained some of their manhood. Our need, therefore, is personal liberation that is tied to the liberation of our men.

In a similar case, a respondent noted that she is interested in women's liberation, but not for the same reasons as white women. For example, she stated, "I do not feel the same oppressions as they do, such as the attitude of down with housework and the domestic scene, but I relate to oppression in the job market." On the other hand, another respondent does not favor the movement, because it has made laws, such as getting alimony and child support harsher, and she would be upset if she had to pay her husband alimony. She does, however, want equal pay for equal work. On the basis of a sample of Black women "conducted through clubs, Hemmons (1980:286,296) supports this finding by noting that "What they (Black women) want is the same economic, job, and educational benefits and opportunities as white males." It appears that the major attraction of Black women, especially Tidewater women, to the women's liberation movement is economics.

Although some respondents were not actively interested in the feminist movement, they still felt a unity with Black women who chose to participate. One respondent, for example, stated, "I'm a true believer in "To each his own, as long as it does not affect others. Therefore, "If Black women desire to join the feminist movement, it is fine with me." Another point of view was noted by a respondent who explained that "Some women join the feminist movement, for they believe that all women are equal." A somewhat different view of a respondent was that they should not work only for sex liberation, but also for race liberation. For example, according to another respondent, "If Black women desire to join the feminist movement, it is their business, but they should not forget about Black liberation." Similarly, another respondent stated, "I do not feel that liberation from sex is the Black woman's main priority, and I am not in full accord with the feminist movement, however, I do not oppose Black women who work for their ideals." These findings indicate that there is no hostility among Tidewater respondents toward Black women who join the women's liberation movement. They also indicate that the views of the respondents toward the women's organization center around why we participate in the movement, the need to focus on race liberation as well as sex liberation, and the opinion that the movement does not adequately meet the needs of Black women. These findings are supported by Hemmons (1980: 297) who noted that "when white women were into consciousness-raising sessions trying to come to grips with whom they were apart from their husbands and children, Black women were seeking groups that would address the issue of massive unemployment and underemployment among Black people in general and Black women specifically. When white women were devising strategies for getting out of the house and into the labor force, vast numbers of Black women were suggesting that they would gladly return home and take care of the home and children if the economic system were not so oppressive on Black men." Nevertheless, the Tidewater respondents indicated that we had at least one need in common with other women. It was liberation from inequality in the workplace, which, was a strong cause for togetherness. These findings also indicate that, in general, the respondents were unified on the notion that we had liberation needs that concerned our households and workplaces.

Unity Among Black Women

The unity of Black women was also seen in communal, social, and civic settings. Although, in a study of Black beauty parlors in Newport News, Virginia, middle class women did not usually seek support in such settings, working and low income women demonstrated unity. They shared information about their problems, illness, and social life with strangers as well as with friends who empathized with them (Barnes 1975:152-153). The beauty parlor operators and clientele were a strong support system for both groups. Similarly, Lorde (1979:52) has noted that "black women have always bonded together in support of each other, however, uneasy and in the face of whatever other allegiances militated against that bonding." The literature of Blacks also indicates that middle class women bind together in social settings; for example, Frazier (1957:222) has noted that they play poker while Barnes (1979:137) has found that they play a great deal of bridge together. By providing an opportunity for conversation and enhancement of self importance, bridge game relationships are important behavior among Black middle class women (Barnes 1979:138). There is also bonding among middle class Black women in civic groups, as demonstrated in Jack and Jill of America, a nationally organized women's group, that focuses on civic and family matters. This organization has 120 chapters or more in thirty three states and the District of Columbia. The chapters are comprised of women who work together to assist other minority children as well as their own adapt in society and contribute to several local and national charities (Barnes 1979:265).

Unkind Behavior Among Black Women

This review of the literature of the family has described the types of behavior among kinswomen and women in the political arena and social organizations. As mentioned earlier in this chapter, the literature describes types of behavior shared by Black women, but it does not adequately inform about the nature of our interpersonal relations. The question that gave impetus to this chapter is whether there is interpersonal interaction that hinders more effective female bonding. Such approach aims to enhance awareness of certain types of female interaction that need to be eliminated for the good of the sex as well as for the good of the race. We obtained such information by asking the Tidewater respondents whether Black women were unkind to each other, operationalized as unkind telephone conversations, criticism, cessation of communication, and failure to cooperate in formal groups unless, of course, their friends were in charge.

Even though the respondents were questioned about all of these aspects of female relations, the major question was whether, in their opinion, Black women were unkind to each other. The data in Table 1 indicate that more than half of the women answering the question agreed that Black women were unkind to one another, but this group included a higher percentage of women under forty (64 percent) than over forty (41 percent). Perhaps younger women have a greater need to vent their frustrations on other women while older women may either have less tension, or they may have learned how to more effectively deal with each other. The alpha value (.01) indicates that a significant relationship exists between the variables.

Table 1

Stressful Behavior among Black Women in Tidewater
By Age of Respondents

Stressful Behavior Occurs among Black Women	Age of Respondents					
	Under 40		Over 40		Total	
	No.	%	No.	%	No.	%
Agree	72	63.7	24	41.4	96	56.1
Disagree	41	36.3	34	58.6	75	43.9
Total	113	66.1	58	33.9	171	100.0

Corrected Chi Square = 6.88606 with 1 degree of freedom
P < 0.0087

The next task was to find out whether tension that develops in management of household and spousal interaction considered in Chapter 3 influence the way Black women interact with each other. To answer this question, as can be seen in Table 2, we asked the women whether there is a relationship between what goes on at home and the nature of interpersonal relations with other Black women in Tidewater. Although the data are not statistically significant, they are informative. Seventy three percent of the sample agreed that there was a relationship between the two variables. The difference between the percentage of women under forty (74 percent) as opposed to the women over forty (70 percent) with this view was miniscule. This finding seems to indicate that our home and community life are woven closely together.

As indicated earlier, in this chapter, we asked the respondents to identify the types of unkind behavior that take place among Black women in Tidewater. The data in Table 3 provide a wide range of unkind behavior among us. When each type was crosstabulated with age, none was found statistically related, unkind conversation excepted; nevertheless, the findings tell us something about the interpersonal

101

Table 2

Spousual Relations Influenced Female Community Behavior
by Age of Respondents

Spouse Relations Impact Female Relations	Age of Respondents					
	Under 40		Over 40		Total	
	No.	%	No.	%	No.	%
Agree	90	74.4	40	70.2	130	73.0
Disagree	31	25.6	17	29.8	48	27.0
Total	121	68.0	57	32.0	178	100.0

relations among Black females. Table 3 shows that the largest percentage of women identified feminine criticism (63 percent), failure to speak and talk with each other (56 percent), and failure to cooperate in social club endeavors (43 percent), unless friends were in charge, as the most frequent types of unkind behavior among Tidewater women. On the other hand, Table 3 does show that only 35 percent of the respondents agreed that we engaged in stressful conversation with other Black women, but almost twice as many women under forty, as over forty, expressed this opinion, a finding supported by the alpha value (.02). This feeling was probably stronger among younger than older women, because they may not have learned when and when not to talk and how to phrase their discontent, or they may have learned how to phrase it, but they had not developed sufficient control to either keep quiet or to speak diplomatically.

Because unkind behavior among Blacks goes as far back as slavery, it is not a new trend in the American society. During slavery, "caste consciousness" and loyalty existed, but the slave community was far from being united. According to Stampp (1963:333), social stratification was a principal factor in the disunity of slaves. It resulted from varied factors, including the social hierarchy created by slave owners. The position of slaves in the hierarchy was determined by tasks performed, and the domestics and artisans were a cut above the field hands (Stampp 1963:333). Besides, slaves who had intimate

Table 3

Reactions to Stressful Treatment of Other
Black Women by Age of Respondents

P a n e l	Reactions	Age of Respondents					
		Under 40		Over 40		Total	
		No.	%	No.	%	No.	%
A	Arguments on Telephone						
	Agree	35	25.5	18	29.5	53	26.8
	Disagree	102	74.5	43	70.5	145	73.2
	Total	137	100.0	61	100.0	198	100.0
B	Criticize Each Other						
	Agree	88	64.2	36	59.0	124	62.6
	Disagree	49	35.8	25	41.0	74	37.4
	Total	137	100.0	61	100.0	198	100.0
C	Quit Speaking and Talking For a Period of Time						
	Agree	76	55.5	34	55.7	110	55.6
	Disagree	61	44.5	27	44.3	88	44.4
	Total	137	100.0	61	100.0	198	100.0
D	Make Harsh Statements In Club Meeting						
	Agree	36	26.3	23	37.7	59	29.8
	Disagree	101	73.7	38	62.3	139	70.2
	Total	137	100.0	61	100.0	198	100.0
E	Fail to Cooperate in Group Endeavors Unless Friends in Charge						
	Agree	62	45.3	24	39.3	86	43.4
	Disagree	75	54.7	37	60.7	112	56.6
	Total	137	100.0	61	100.0	198	100.0
F	Engage in Stressful Conversation						
	Agree	55	40.1	14	23.0	69	34.8
	Disagree	82	59.9	47	77.0	129	65.2
	Total	137	69.2	61	30.8	198	100.0

Panel F:
      Corrected Chi Square = 4.76528 with 1 degree of freedom
      P < 0.0290

103

contact with their master imitated his manners and performed personal services for him had more prestige in the social hierarchy than other slaves. Additionally, the fortune to be owned by a master with great wealth and social prestige and possession of a light skin complexion also led to social differentiation (Stampp 1963:338,339). Unkind behavior did not disappear with emancipation, thus, during the early forties, as noted in Chapter 1, there was antagonism in and between social classes. An example of the latter occurred when low income parents would not cooperate in the Colored PTA under the leadership of an upper class person (Davis and the Gardners 1941:210). Hence, the origin of unkind behavior among Blacks can be traced back to slavery and the first half of this century. Nonetheless, it is not justifiable.

Dyadic Behavior of Black Women

Because a majority of the women agreed that there were at least five types of unkind behavior among Black women in Tidewater, we asked the women in the follow up sample to describe the unpleasant relations among us. The analysis indicates that they occurred mainly in dyads, however, at times, one or both members of the dyad had a support group. Further analysis of the data indicates that unkind treatment among us was centered mainly around three issues, jealousy, children's relations, and men.

We asked the respondents several questions about female jealousy in Tidewater. Their replies indicate that jealousy among us was a source of harsh female behavior. This is probably the case, a respondent stated, because "we hate, with a passion to see each other succeed." The replies of the Tidewater respondents also indicate that we are jealous of job titles, promotions, physical appearance, furniture, cars, homes, and our men. A respondent who had lived in several working and lower middle class and low rent project areas had found that women in housing projects begrudge each other more than other women. When asked why, she noted that it results from being "trapped in an undesirable environment and not able to see our way out." Because material achievements seem to result in jealousy among Black women in Tidewater, Black leaders here could accomplish a great deal. They could encourage healthy middle age persons, as well as young persons, to not only work but become the best workers. When there are no jobs, we could be taught to put the community on alert that we are honest and hard working people who desire to earn our keep. Until such a time as more Blacks in low income areas are gainfully employed, jealousy may continue as a major issue in Black women's relations in Tidewater. Of course, according to the respondents, mutual female jealousy among Black women had no boundaries. It was found, they say, among middle class women, especially in women's groups, and could be as devastating as jealousy in other social classes.

Another major issue in female relations was centered around children's experiences. According to the respondents, we expended a lot of energy solving our children's problem. Unkind relations, about children's problems occurred among us when one mother approached another mother about her child's behavior. According to a respondent, our Tidewater children threatened others by telling them that if things did not go their way, their Mama would beat their Mama, and a number of children in Tidewater housing projects made good their threats. Without getting both sides of the story, we engaged each other in arguments. This usually meant that the mother of the defeated child threatened that, if such behavior happened again, she would take punitive actions, such as whipping the woman or taking her to court. While we were arguing, other women and children gathered to listen and watch. Such matches dramatized in harsh voice tones and body gestures, were a source of neighborhood entertainment, evident in our children's comments to late comers, "You missed a good one!" It is likely that our women engaged in such duels for a number of reasons, including stress. Perhaps it resulted from enormous material and emotional deprivation as well as the hopelessness of our circumstances. Besides, verbal matches were likely to satisfy certain needs, such as status and attention. Indeed, we need more productive outlets, such as good jobs, hard work, and good pay, and strong emotional bonds with men and women to achieve a sense of status and hinder loss of self esteem.

Although verbal matches among Tidewater women may satisfy certain needs, it is likely that our reactions to our children's problems inadvertently socialize them in the same types of behavior, which probably helps perpetuate female duels as an intricate element of interaction in some low rent housing areas. As shown in Chapter 1, this finding is somewhat supported by Davis and Gardner (1941) who found that upper class adolescent cliques modeled their behavior after upper class adults. Perhaps, however, training children in ways to act harshly toward other women reached a peak when one mother took another mother to court. According to a respondent, our children were usually willing to resume play a short time after fights, but we took their disagreements more seriously. For example, the respondent reported that while a particular mother was at the courthouse taking out a warrant against the mother whose child had beaten her child, the children started playing again. When the mother returned home, she became angry and beat her child for reestablishing the friendship. This means that, for some of us, our children's fights were a double problem. The situation was compounded by the justice system, because, according to a respondent, the judge often ruled in favor of the woman whose children inflicted marks on other children and reprimanded the complainants. It appeared that the ruling was aimed at keeping our women out of court more than at teaching us how and why we should become less involved in our children's disputes and fights.

If the aim of the judge was to reduce the number of such cases, he was, indeed, successful. For example, when a mother, in Tidewater, disapproved of the judge's ruling, she told him that if her child got beaten again, she would handle the situation. Though children seemed to take their disputes and fights less seriously than their mothers, it was likely that they learned the entire spectrum of abusive behavior from them, a practice that, as stated earlier, may perpetuate the system. It appears that such expenditure of time and energy on children's problems has some other consequences. It may be that it causes women to neglect the upkeep of their homes and supervision of their children's school homework. Moreover, when mothers have erroneously "sided with them," it is likely to be more difficult to discipline children. Again, community leaders have a great opportunity to help us transfer our energies from relatively useless endeavors to those that count, such as job preparation, employment, and job excellence, and mutual female love and companionship.

Further, we also found that men are another source of stress in Black female behavior and it, too, occurred mainly in dyadic contexts. Similar to children, as seen in Chapter 3, we used a great deal of time and energy attempting to prevent other women from gaining access to our husbands or attempting to gain access to other women's husbands. The result was that one woman abused another or there was mutual stress in female behavior. An example is one of our women who attempted to obtain the companionship of a respondent's husband. In this case, the "other woman" harassed her lover's wife by calling her names on the telephone, as well as by visiting her home, in the middle of the night, to take the man to her home. When the woman arrived, a particular night, holding a crowbar, she said to the man's wife, "You come out and I am coming in." The wife swung the door open, as if it had no hinges and, with appropriate expletives, invited her inside the house. The "other woman" accepted the invitation, but the wife also remained in the home, and her husband chose to stay with her rather than accompany his lover. As easily seen, this case involved several types of unkind behavior, including unkind voice

106

tones, harsh statements, and telephone arguments. Beyond this, the "Other woman" did not receive the companionship of her lover and tension between spouses may have had the same effect on the wife. We must also point out that jealousy among neighbors as well as jealousy over men is self-inflicted pain. What likely happens is that both women, in this type of situation, experience lower self-esteem, along with a great deal of frustration, while the man's self-esteem may be inflated. Perhaps our jealousy can be contained a number of ways, including teaching young children, boys and girls, to develop a positive self concept that makes such inflicted pain unnecessary and by teaching young married couples that extramarital relations are painful affairs that weaken the family bond, especially the marital bond. When such relationship is discovered, it often drains the marital bond of affection, warmth, and emotion, the cement that makes marriage worthwhile. Besides, they should be taught that extramarital pairing is often a consequence of something missing in the marriage and, therefore, each spouse should work toward growth and enhancement of each other along with the development of some freedom that does not keep a man or woman imprisoned.

Clique Behavior

Cliques were another pattern of behavior among Black women in Tidewater. However, it is not a new form of behavior, for example, in the 1940s and 1950s, there were cliques in and between social classes. According to Kardiner and Ovesey (1962), small clubs and cliques were "Torn asunder by the mutual antagonism, rivalries, and the quest for leadership and prestige." Similarly, clique behavior among Black women in Tidewater was still a problem in social and civic organizations. One such example occurred in a social and civic group where the president sought advice, but made her own decisions. A small group of women, regardless of the person elected to the presidency, had been accustomed to "managing the organization." When they found they could no longer dominate it nor hold all the major committee chairmenships, initially, they created disturbance by speaking harshly to a few members. But, as time went on, and the president followed a course of action that benefitted the entire organization, the clique redirected its antagonism to the president. This means that at least two of the clique members often made long and demeaning speeches criticizing the actions of the president, and the remainder of the clique members played a supportive role by making short cutting remarks to the president, immediately after the meetings, or by asking questions and introducing side issues that delayed the meetings and created problems whose resolutions sometimes required two additional meetings. By the time the president completed her term, the small, but powerful clique, had divided the more than 100 members, and the division was demonstrated in voting behavior and seating at the meetings. Besides, friends in the clique, on the day of election of new officers, entered with smiles and other facial expressions that gave an accurate preview of the outcome of the meeting and election.

The president did not retaliate, but she was hurt and frustrated, evident in telephone calls. Furthermore, following meetings, it usually took several hours for her to go to sleep. In fact, the tension in the meetings became extremely tense, and, on one such occasion, a member went home and told her husband that she was withdrawing from active membership, for the meetings left her virtually ill. She kept her promise and many other women followed her action, but it was not an action the women desired. It thus appears that cliques in formal settings impede organizational progress, deprive us of club memberships and attendance at club meetings, and contribute to personal and emotional stress and strain. Another dimension of cliques in some Tidewater organizations was that they comprised mini-clubs whose members developed a close relationship. Their committee meetings were social gatherings where members ate, drank, talked, and laughed heartily, shared information, made committee plans, and decided their actions for the general meetings. Besides, even when some groups appeared congenial, their membership often left the general meetings depressed and disturbed over the lack of democratic procedures and apparent clique domination. It thus seems that members in organizations realized that protest against what went on in meetings would make them outcasts: hence, the best course to take was either, remain silent or make remarks that conformed to the thinking of the dominant clique. On rare occasions, however, a woman registered her dissent, but often, not without reprisals.

These findings about dyadic and clique behavior indicate that, regardless of social class, we were open to slights and verbal attacks from our own women. However, it appears that among low income women they were more likely to occur in personal encounters while among middle class women they were likely to occur in voluntary associations. This difference may result in part from the relatively limited participation of low income women in voluntary associations and the infrequent face to face dyadic contact of Black middle class women.

Reactions to Stress in Black Female Relations

The Tidewater respondents were asked to identify the reactions of

Table 4

Reactions to Stressful Behavior among Black Women
by Age of Respondents

P a n e l	Reactions	Age of Respondents					
		Under 40		Over 40		Total	
		No.	%	No.	%	No.	%
A	Talk and Socialize Only With Women Known to be Friendly Toward Them						
	Agree	97	66.7	35	53.8	132	62.9
	Disagree	48	33.1	30	46.2	78	37.1
	Total	145	69.0	65	31.0	210	100.0
B	Withdrawal From Voluntary Groups						
	Agree	76	52.4	35	53.8	111	52.9
	Disagree	69	47.6	30	46.2	99	47.1
	Total	145	69.0	65	31.0	210	100.0
C	Return Unkind Words and Actions						
	Agree	97	66.9	43	66.2	140	66.7
	Disagree	48	33.1	22	33.8	70	33.3
	Total	140	69.0	65	31.0	210	100.0

Black women to unkind behavior of other Black women. In Table 4, we examined the reactions among Black women in Tidewater to such behavior. It indicates that they reacted three ways to unkind treatment, but when each variable was cross-tabulated with the age of the respondents, none was found significant. However, Table 4 does show that the findings are informative. According to the respondents, we reacted to unkind behavior of other women by returning unkind words and actions (67 percent), socializing only with women known to be friendly (63 percent), and withdrawing from voluntary associations (53 percent). Moreover, it is possible that all reactions were manifested by women on varied social class levels, but the tendency to return unkind words and actions may be less intense among middle class than working and low income women.

A Critical Need

The findings in this chapter seem to suggest the urgency of female bonding among nonkinswomen. Such bond would tie together all of our Black women in Tidewater, regardless of social standing, in a common relationship that affords respect, freedom, and love for all. Such achievement would not only be a first step to improved relations with our men, but with men and women in the larger society.

REFERENCES CITED

Barnes, Annie S.
1975   "The Black Beauty Parlor Complex in A Southern City."
        PHYLON 36:149-154.

Barnes, Annie S.
1979   "An Urban Voluntary Association." PHYLON XL: 264-269.

Barnes, Annie S.
1979   "Voluntary Association Participation" TENNESSEE ANTHRO-
        POLOGIST IV:129-139.

Barnes, Annie S.
1981   "The Black Kinship System." PHYLON XLII:369-380.

Barnes, Annie S.
1983   "Black Husbands and Wives: An Assessment of Marital
        Roles in A Middle Class Neighborhood." In Constance E.
        Obudho (ed.) CONTEMPORARY BLACK MARRIAGES
        AND FAMILY LIFE. Westport: Greenwood Press, pp. 55-73.

Brink, William and Louis Harris
1964   THE NEGRO REVOLUTION. New York: Simon & Schuster.

Brown, Hallie Q.
1971   HOMESPUN HEORINES AND OTHER WOMEN OF DISTINC-
        TION. Freeport: Books for Libraries Press

Davis, Allison and Burleigh B. and Mary R. Gardner
1941   DEEP SOUTH. Chicago: The University of Chicago Press.

Dollard, John
1937   CASTE AND CLASS IN A SOUTHERN TOWN. New York:
        Doubleday & Company

Dows, Karl E.
1943   MEET THE NEGRO. Pasadena: The Login Press.

Drake, St. Clair and Horace R. Cayton
1945   BLACK METROPOLIS, II. New York: Harper and Row, Publishers.

Dubois, W.E.B.
1898   SOME EFFECTS OF AMERICAN NEGROES FOR THEIR BETTERMENT. Atlanta: Atlanta University Press.

Frazier, E. Franklin
1957   BLACK BOURGEOISIE. New York: The Free Press.

Hemmons, Willa Mae
1980   "The Women's Liberation Movement: Understanding Black Women's Attitudes." In La Frances Rodgers-Rose (ed.) THE BLACK WOMAN. Beverly Hills: Sage Publications.

Jack, Lenus, Jr.
1978   "Kinship and Residential Propinquity in Black New Orleans: The Wesleys." In Demitri B. Shimkin, et al. (eds.) THE EXTENDED FAMILY IN BLACK SOCIETIES. The Hague: Mouton Publishers, pp. 239-269.

Johnson, Charles
1941   GROWING UP IN THE BLACK BELT. New York: Schocken Books.

Kardiner, Abraham and Lionel Ovesey
1962   THE MARK OF OPPRESSION. New York: The World Publishing Company.

Ladner, Joyce
1972   TOMORROW'S TOMORROW. Garden City: Doubleday & Company.

Lerner, Gerda
1972   BLACK WOMEN IN WHITE AMERICA. New York: Vintage Books.

Lorde, Audre
1979   "We Need Only Look at the Close, Highly Complex, and Involved Relationships Between African Co-Wives. . ." MS. MAGAZINE 7:52,70.

Lowenberg, James and Ruth Bogin
1976 BLACK WOMEN IN NINETEENTH CENTURY AMERICAN LIFE. University Park: The Pennsylvania State University Press.

MacIver, R. M.
1970 THE SOCIETY. Chicago: The University of Chicago Press.

Martin, Elmer P. and Joanne Mitchell Martin
1978 THE BLACK EXTENDED FAMILY. Chicago: The University of Chicago Press.

McAdoo, Harriett Pipes
1979 "Black Kinship," PSYCHOLOGY TODAY 12:67,69,70,79,110.

Reid, Inez Smith
1972 "TOGETHER" BLACK WOMEN. New York: Emerson Hall Publishers, Inc.

Rodgers-Rose La Frances
1980 THE BLACK WOMAN. Beverly Hills: Sage Publications.

Rollins, Charlemagne Hill
1964 THEY SHOWED THE WAY. New York: Thomas Y. Crowell Company.

Ross, John C. and Raymond H. Wheeler
1971 BLACK BELONGING. Westport: Greenwood Publishing Co.

Shimkin, Demitri B. et al.
1978 "The Black Extended Family: A Basic Rural Institution and A Mechanism of Urban Adaptation." In Demitri B. Shimkin et al. (eds.) THE EXTENDED BLACK FAMILY IN BLACK SOCIETIES. The Hague: Mouton Publishers, pp. 25-147.

Slaby, Andrew E. and Joan R. Sealy
1973 "Black Liberation, Women's Liberation." AMERICAN JOURNAL OF PSYCHOLOGY 130:196-199.

Stack, Carol B.
1974 ALL OUR KIN. New York: Harper and Row, Publishers.

Stampp, Kenneth M.
  1963   THE PECULIAR INSTITUTION. New York: Alfred A. Knopf.

Staples, Robert
  1973   THE BLACK WOMAN IN AMERICA. Chicago: Nelson
          Hall Publishers.

Tumin, Melvin
  1967   SOCIAL STRATIFICATION. Englwood Cliffs: Prentice-Hall,
          Inc.

CHAPTER FIVE

SUMMARY

Introduction

Our explorations into and analysis of stress in interpersonal relations of Black women led us in many directions. In particular, we asked how Black women in our sample and their friends in Tidewater are faring in the environments -- the workplace, home, and community -- that are essential to daily life. We were interested in the types of stressful conditions experienced in each setting, the causes of such conditions, and their impact on Black women. The purpose of these inquiries was to illuminate our understanding of Black women and, hopefully, effect a stronger bond among ourselves, our men and ourselves, white women and ourselves, and the entire society and ourselves.

We began this analysis in Chapter 1 with a review of the literature about the interpersonal relations of Blacks. It indicates that, in the mid thirties and forties, the interpersonal relations between whites and Blacks were contradictory and sometimes antagonistic. This analysis also suggests that, in the Black community, the interpersonal relations were a mirror image of the relations between whites and Blacks. Clearly, there were multiple factors in the stressful relations among our people; for example, they did not get along well, because of disagreements rooted in skin color, use of a derogatory term of address, and the attitudes of the upper caste toward the lower caste (Davis and the Gardners 1941:21,24). Also, when husbands and wives did not get along, because of white intervention, the home mirrored the problems between whites and Blacks; moreover, the interpersonal relations among siblings of different complexions probably were also antagonistic.

On the other hand, the research in Chapter 1 also indicates that there were two trends in interpersonal relations between the sixties and eighties. One trend addressed the loving relationships in Black marriages while the second trend replicated the difficulty found in earlier marriages. Both trends indicate that the literature of Blacks, since the early sixties, has begun to discuss the interpersonal relations in Black marriages. This is a step forward in obtaining more knowledge about our family that will probably lessen stress in our homes as we continue the struggle to overcome sex and racial barriers in the environments. This study expanded this trend by analyzing the interpersonal relations of Black women in the workplace, home, and community in the framework of four independent variables: age, sex, employer preference, and occupation of respondents.

The Workplace

The findings in the literature had settled the issue that job discrimination occurs in the work environment. They indicate that a number of actors -- employers, employees, customers, and educational institutions -- discriminate against us directly or indirectly, but there were no empirical findings about the effects of discrimination and job protest. Along with this gap in the literature, as also noted in Chapters 1 and 2, there is virtually no empirical research about employer preferences and employer relations of Black women.

We therefore, determined the employer preferences[*] of the respondents in the Tidewater sample. As expected, some respondents preferred working for each employer type. Another expectation was that a statistically significant relationship would exist between age of respondents and each employer preference. This expectation was not supported; instead, we found that employer preference data, by age of respondents, indicated that, collectively, race, sex and age were significantly related to employer choice. Hence, the respondents in both age categories preferred white employers more often than Black employers and male employers rather than female employers.

Our next expectation was that some employers would be stronger on interpersonal relations than other employers. It seems that white male employers were more complimentary on job performance and stronger on compatibility with the Tidewater respondents than other employers. At the same time, white female employers demonstrated more equality in employer-employee relations and expressed more thanks for the work of the Tidewater respondents than other employers. Also, the white employers expressed more thanks than Black employers, but, Black employers were friendlier toward Tidewater respondents

[*]White males, White females, Black Males, Black females

115

than white employers. Thus, our data supported our expectation that employers varied in the expression of interpersonal qualities to the respondents.

When the interpersonal relations between Black female employers and employees were analyzed in greater depth, we found some additional dimensions, including the perceptions they had of each other. The respondents noted that Black female employers believed that Black female employees did not perform domestic duties and work efficiently for Black women. They also had the opinion that Black female employees resented Black female employers and were jealous of their standing in the workplace. At the same time, the respondents believed that Black female employees considered the work assignments given by Black female employers heavy and their conversation harsh. Nevertheless, it appears that there was an underlying closeness between Black female employers and Black employees. It was evident in the desire of employees to obtain more work consideration from their Black female counterparts than from other female employers.

Our next expectation was that employers would vary on the manifestation of interpersonal characteristics by occupation of respondents. On the compatibility quality, we thus found that male employers and white female employers were more alike than Black female employers and other employer types. Hence, they were more compatible with respondents high up in the occupational structure while Black female employers were more compatible with respondents lower in the occupational structure. Therefore, the data support our expectation that employers varied by occupation in the expression of compatibility to the respondents.

On the expression of equality in the workplace, there was also variation by preferred employer and occupation of respondents. Of the respondents who preferred white female employers, a larger percentage in service type jobs, such as social and domestic work, experienced equality in their relations than in nonservice type occupations, teaching excepted. Among the respondents who preferred Black female employers, teachers and social workers experienced equality in work relations more often than other respondents while the respondents who preferred Black male employers and experienced relations of equality were administrators and nurses. Similarly, of the respondents who preferred white male employers, administrators and social workers experienced relations of equality more often than other employees. Hence, a high status among the respondents in the occupational structure was usually associated with equality between them and their employers.

We found that friendliness in employer-employee relations also varied by employer type and occupation of respondents. The major finding is that Black employers were friendlier than white employers to the respondents, but the Black male employers were friendlier toward administrators and nurses than other respondents while the Black female employers were friendlier toward clerical and social workers. Similar to Black male and Black female employers, white male employers expressed friendliness to administrators and social workers more often than to other respondents. Also, the female employers were similar; for example, white female employers showed more friendliness toward teachers and domestic workers and Black female employers showed more friendliness toward social and clerical workers.

There is also evidence that employees in Tidewater varied by occupation in the expression of appreciation for tasks performed. The data indicate that white females expressed thanks more often to the respondents highest and lowest in the occupational structure, administrators and domestic workers, while white male employers expressed more thanks to service type workers, nurses, secretaries, and domestics. Similarly, Black female employers expressed more thanks to service type workers, social workers and secretaries, and Black male employers expressed more thanks to teachers, a traditional professional group, among Blacks, and social workers, a service type group. Clearly, the employers not only varied by race and sex, but also by occupation. Nevertheless, a majority of the employers expressed thanks to service type workers more often than to teachers and administrators. The data also indicate that white employers thanked the respondents for tasks accomplished more often than Black employers.

It follows that white male and Black female employers complimented service type workers more frequently than other respondents while white female employers gave more compliments to service type workers and administrators and Black male employers complimented social workers and teachers more frequently than other respondents. The evidence also indicates that male employers were more complimentary on tasks performed by the respondents than female employers.

Empirical evidence in Chapter 2 also indicates that the Tidewater respondents experienced discrimination in the workplace. We thus expected that they varied in job discrimination by employer type and their occupational afiliation. A related expectation was that types of job discrimination would be significantly related to age of respondents. However, similar to interpersonal relations, only two types of discrimination were significantly related to age of respondents.

We thus found that a larger percentage of the respondents under forty than over forty had been assigned fewer jobs with higher duties while a higher percentage of the women over forty than under forty had not gotten a raise on time. Although other types of job discrimination were not found significantly related to employer type and occupational affiliation, like age, the data helped us understand the experiences of the Tidewater respondents in the workplace.

One type of job discrimination was difficulty in obtaining employment. The analysis indicates that the Tidewater respondents had this experience less frequently with Black female and male employers. Similarly, when we compared the respondents in varied occupations, who preferred each employer type, we found some variations. For example, a larger percentage of administrators than other employees failed to get jobs with both types of female employers. On the other hand, the largest percentage of the respondents who preferred white male employers and Black male employers and failed to get employment were in social work. Further, there was very little difference between the percentage of administrators and social workers denied employment by all employer types.

The Tidewater respondents also experienced problems on their jobs, such as work assignments. We found that a larger percentage of the respondents who preferred white female employers and Black male employers had not been assigned jobs with higher duties than respondents who preferred white male employers and Black female employers. Consequently, the white female employers and Black male employers were more alike than employers of the same race. We also found that, of the respondents who preferred white employers, the percentage of respondents who had not been assigned jobs with higher duties was almost three times greater for women over forty than women under forty.

By occupation and employer preference, we also found some variation among employer types. For example, the largest percentage of the respondents who preferred white female employers and were not assigned jobs with higher duties were employed in social and clerical work while the respondents who preferred Black female employers and had this experience were in administration and social work. On the other hand, of the respondents who preferred white male employers, the largest percentage not assigned jobs with higher duties were teachers and clerical workers, but the largest percentage of the respondents who preferred Black male employers with this experience were in social and clerical work. Moreover, social and clerical workers com-

118

prised two groups that failed most often to be assigned jobs with higher duties by all employer types.

The next type of job discrimination, assignment of too much work, also varied by employer type. We found that white employers assigned too much work more frequently than Black employers, and male employers assigned too much work more often than female employers. Similarly, there was variation by occupation and employer preference. White female employers tended to assign social workers and nurses too much work while white male employers assigned nurses and administrators too much work. Similarly, Black male employers assigned too much work to nurses and social workers while Black female employers assigned too much work to nurses and clerical workers. Hence, a larger percentage of all employer types had assigned the respondents in nursing too much work.

The next job related problem, long work hours, also indicates variation by employer type. However, the respondents who preferred white female employers and Black male employers had this experience more often than the respondents who preferred white male and Black female employers. The variation by occupation and employer preference was also noticeable. Of the respondents who preferred white female employers, the highest percentage with this experience was in administration and social work while the largest percentage of respondents with this experience and preferred Black male employers was in administration and nursing. A higher percentage of the respondents in administration was assigned long work hours by white female and Black male employers. The highest percentage that preferred white male employers and assigned long work hours was in nursing and administration. Similarly, the highest percentage of the respondents who preferred Black female employers with this experience was in social work and nursing. However, the administrators who preferred white employers and Black male employers had been assigned long work hours more often than the respondents who preferred Black female employers. We next found that receipt of low wages was also a problem faced by the Tidewater respondents. It is concluded that the respondents who preferred female employers received low wages more frequently than respondents who preferred male employers. There was also variation by employer preference and occupation. Of the respondents who preferred white employers and Black male employers, the administrators and social workers received low wages more frequently than other respondents while those who preferred Black female employers and recieved low wages most frequently were administrators and nurses. In general, a larger percentage of

119

administrators and social workers received low wages than respondents in other occupations. This analysis also indicates that the white female and Black male employers were more similar and the Black female and white male employers were more similar than same race employers on this variable. In effect, there was a cross-sex principle as well as a transracial principle involved in the receipt of low wages.

Another finding is that the respondents experienced not receiving a raise. The findings indicate that white employers were more than twice as likely to fail to give the respondents raises than Black employers. Nevertheless, by occupation, all employer types failed to give respondents in service type occupations a raise more often than other respondents.

A related problem experienced by the Tidewater respondents was that they did not receive a raise on time. The findings suggest that the respondents who preferred white employers were more likely not to get a raise on time than respondents who preferred Black employers. Likewise, the respondents who preferred female employers were more likely not to get a raise on time than the respondents who preferred male employers. Hence, the sex and race of the Tidewater employers influenced the frequency that the respondents did not get a raise on time. By occupation, we found that a larger percentage of all employer types failed to give service type workers a raise on time more often than other respondents.

The final type of job discrimination described by the Tidewater respondents was slow promotions. The respondents who preferred female employers experienced slow promotions more often than other respondents who preferred male employers. Further, the respondents in all occupational categories, by employer types, had experienced not getting a promotion on time, but the experience was known less often by the respondents in varied occupations who preferred Black male employers than by respondents who preferred other employer types.

These findings about the interpersonal relations and job discrimination experienced by the respondents in Tidewater tell us a great deal about their experience in the work environment. Most signficantly, they indicate that white employers ranked higher than Black employers on interpersonal relations while Black employers ranked higher than white employers on job benefits in the workplace. The findings also suggest that administrators and social workers had a more difficult time with interpersonal relations and job discrimination than other respondents. It thus appears that the respondents in the middle range of the occupational scale, especially teachers, fared better on interpersonal relations and job discrimination in the workplace than other respondents. Further, the findings in this study indicate that in general male and female employers were about even on the expression of interpersonal relations to the respondents, but the male employers ranked higher than female employers on job benefits.

Because we found that the Tidewater respondents had experienced job discrimination, we asked them whether they had protested. They informed us that, instead of protesting, some respondents endured it, quit work, or worked until they could find another job. As expected, some of the respondents also protested against job discrimination. Their protest mechanisms included discussions and arguments with employers, written complaints, unpleasant attitudes, and gossip, but they were not significantly related to employer type. Table 20 in Chapter 2 does show that gossip in the workplace is significantly related to age of respondents, for a larger percentage of older than younger respondents used it as a means of protesting job discrimination. There was also variation by employer type on the use made of these mechanisms. Concerning discussions, we found that a higher percentage of the respondents who preferred Black employers discussed job related problems than respondents who preferred other employers; however, a higher percentage of the respondents who preferred male employers used discussions than respondents who preferred female employers. Similarly, the Tidewater respondents gossiped more frequently about male than female employers, and 50 percent of the respondents who gossiped about Black male employers were over forty years of age. On the other hand, a larger percentage of the respondents who preferred white employers used written complaints, arguments, and unpleasant attitudes to protest discrimination than respondents who preferred Black employers.

There were benefits derived from all employer types. Of the respondents who preferred white female and male employers, the highest percentage received an improved attitude while the largest percentage who preferred Black female employers received a reduced work load. Again, we found that the results received from white employers and Black male employers were very much alike while the benefits received from Black female employers were dissimilar. Throughout this analysis of the workplace, the female employers often differed from male employers while, in other cases, they were similar to these employers, especially white males. Although the findings indicate that the benefits were related to employer type, they suggest that Tidewater respondents had experienced a degree of success in overcoming problems in the workplace. Similarly, the findings make clear that some workplaces in Tidewater made provision for employee relief from job discrimination by allowing the respondents to protest to immediate supervisors and obtain benefits.

We also asked the respondents whether they protested discrimination to the supervisors of the immediate employers and whether they received more results from one race of supervisors than another. They reported that Black supervisors of employers gave about the same amount of justice in complaints as white supervisors of immediate employers. As would be expected, the findings also indicate that a larger percentage of the Tidewater respondents complained to the supervisors of Black employers than to the supervisors of white employers. In all probability, some of the supervisors of white and Black employers were of their same race; hence, in both instances, less justice may have been anticipated. Moreover, a larger percentage of the respondents who preferred male employers protested to their supervisors than respondents who preferred female employers.

The Home

As Nelson (1975) has noted, work has always been "the basic economic function for the survival of the Black family." Thus, as shown in Chapter 3, we found that, like the slave family, the Black family, in the mid 1930s and early 1940s, and the Black bourgeoisie family, Tidewater families worked. What else is common to all these families is that their wages did not enable them to adequately manage the necessities of life, including good housing, the Black bourgeoisie and modern middle class family excepted. Upon finding that families in Tidewater often lacked an adequate home environment, we determined the quality of their marriage relations. We found that 91 percent of the respondents perceived Black marriages in Tidewater as stressful.

Several categories of marital behavior, including employment, were used to understand stress in Black marriages. The 148 married respondents were asked how their spouses reacted to their employment. Clearly more than 60 percent of the husbands of the respondents wanted them to work. Correspondingly, the women enjoyed working, however, because the money was needed to help support the household, they also found work stressful. The problem was that they did not like being pressured to work. Two related questions were whether the husbands of the Tidewater respondents enjoyed seeing them receive good wages and promotions. We found that a large percentage of the respondents' husbands liked to see them get good wages while an overwhelming majority of their husbands desired them to get promotions, but a larger percentage of the women over forty than under forty were married to men favorable toward their promotions. We concluded that Black marriages in Tidewater were relatively stress free, on all counts, regarding wife employment, except the necessity to work.

Moreover, the findings indicate that the Tidewater respondents obtained intrinsic satisfaction from employment. For example, an overwhelming majority (85 percent) preferred working to staying at home, and a few respondents worked to keep from getting bored; of the latter group, a larger percentage of the respondents under forty than over forty worked to keep from getting bored. Similarly, only a small percentage of the women in both age categories worked to get inspiration to do household tasks. Conversely, a large percentage of the respondents in both age categories reported that working made them feel good about themselves. It follows that the percentage of Tidewater respondents who agreed that working made them feel guilty and less feminine was negligible. Even though the respondents did not like to work, because their money was needed to help sustain the household, it is clear that they derived immense satisfaction from work.

The Tidewater respondents also noted that they derived extrinsic satisfaction from working. For example, a large percentage of the women in both age categories said that working contributed to their personal and household economic security and gave them an opportunity to make personal purchases. Also, the respondents, especially the women over forty, obtained money to educate their children, and a small percentage of them worked to accumulate savings. In view of the stress experienced in the workplace, we expected to find that another type of extrinsic satisfaction from employment would be recreation. Surprisingly, only a small percentage of the respondents worked to obtain money for recreation. This may indicate that, in general, the recreation of Black couples was still family oriented, and that Black middle class recreation was both family and community oriented. Also, this finding may suggest that most of their income was needed to sustain the household.

Because essentials basic to existence consumed much of the Tidewater respondents' income, we determined the importance of their spouses's paychecks. According to the respondents, the use that some husbands made of their own paycheck caused stress in our marriages. An overwhelming majority of the respondents agreed that it occurred when our husbands failed to bring all or the necessary part of their paycheck home to support our households. Stress in Tidewater marriages resulting from husbands' paychecks took many forms, including arguments and fights. Both effects were known more frequently by the women over forty than under forty. Because a relatively small percentage of the respondents agreed that the use husbands made of their own paychecks led to fights, perhaps characteristically it did not lead to physical violence in Black marriages in Tidewater. Two other results of marital stress resulting from husbands' use of their paycheck were that it was usually the woman who borrowed money to tide the family over until the next pay day, and, less frequently than all other results, it caused marital separation.

The literature in Chapter 3 has shown that matrifocality, equalitarianism, and patriarchy are authority patterns in Black marriages. The respondents noted that wife dominance was the pattern that caused stress in Tidewater marriages. Sixty-six percent of the respondents agreed that our husbands' role in the decision making process needed to be improved, but the respondents under forty noted this finding more often than respondents over forty.

Because we found that extent of husband participation in decision making caused marital stress, we determined the reaction of wives to it. A small percentage of the respondents, especially the women under forty, noted that it led to separation. Some other respondents said that wives reacted to low husband participation in the decision making process by implementing decisions and informing their husbands, or making decisions unbeknowing to them. In both cases, the pattern obtained more often among women under than over forty. Another indication of stress in Tidewater marriages from low husband participation in decision making was spousal arguments, however, a slightly larger percentage of the women over forty than under forty noted this result. Of course, another dimension to low husband participation in the decision making process focused on husbands' attitude toward family problems. According to the Tidewater respondents, they held women responsible for their occurrence, but younger respondents noted this husband reaction more frequently than women over forty.

The respondents reported that some Tidewater marriages experienced stress, because husbands lacked skills in making household repairs. However, only a third of the respondents reported that lack of such skill caused stress in Tidewater marriages, a finding noted more often by younger than older women.

Starting with slavery, some Black marriages have been characterized by affection while others have needed a stronger emotional bond. The literature (Scanzoni, 1971) also supports the finding that Black women desire a strong emotional bond with their spouse. Even though this may be the case, as mentioned earlier, our data indicate that 91 percent of the respondents agreed that husbands in Tidewater treated their wives unkindly. As a result of this finding, we determined the nature of such treatment. A large percentage of the respondents agreed that our men did not give us love, warmth, and affection, but this opinion was held more often among women over than under forty. As a result, in the opinion of 100 percent of the respondents in both age categories, we reacted by manifesting tension in spousal interpersonal relations. Another finding is that we felt insecure and unloved when our husbands were unkind, a finding noted more often by the women over forty than by the women under forty; nevertheless, almost 100 percent of the women in both age groups agreed that we reacted that way.

Also, a large percentage of the respondents, especially the women under forty, agreed that another type of husband behavior in Tidewater was unfaithfulness. It took several forms: the trio arrangement, group arrangement, and an economic and sexual arrangement. However, it was the latter that caused most stress in marriage relations; it caused us to react a number of ways.

A relatively small percentage of the respondents reported that we reacted to husband unfaithfulness by showing jealousy and suspicion of other women. The respondents described the indicators of this reaction. According to these findings, we disliked our husbands looking into the eyes of other women, at least for sustained periods of time, dancing too much, or on slow musical numbers with them, and holding their hands, during introductions. Moreover, we also reacted by arguing and fighting our husbands, refusing to talk and sleep with them, and by taking a lover.

It was concluded that, if our Tidewater husbands gave us more love, warmth, and affection, and refrained from love affairs with other women, our marriages would be happier. It was also concluded that extramarital relations, experienced by Black women in Tidewater, are by necessity rather than by choice. Another conclusion is that, if our husbands refrained from marital weakness, we would be happier women in the community, because our relations with our spouses spill over into other environments, especially the community.

The Community

After the Tidewater women worked and managed their households, they had a limited amount of time for participation in religious, civic, and social activities. As shown in Chapter 4, the origin of our voluntary association participation began during slavery and continued until the present, and a majority of our community activities were with other women. Consequently, this section of the summary concerns interpersonal relations among Black women. As background information, we found that one type of relationship among Black women was kin behavior (see Chapter 4). Kinswomen communicated with each other, shared family occasions, and provided financial assistance, advice, shelter, food, clothing, services and emotional support for one another. Although there was some stress in the relationships (Stack 1970; Barnes 1981; McAdoo 1979), there was unity among Black kinswomen. The unity among non-kinswomen was less well known, yet we do know that they participated in efforts to obtain freedom for our race and sex (Brown 1971; Lerner 1972; Lowenberg and Bogin 1976; Rollins 1964). the unity of Black women has also been seen in social groups (Frazier 1957; Barnes 1979) and civic groups (Barnes 1979). Taking the lead from this literature, it is clear that Black women interacted with each other and, thus, the primary question here focused on the quality of bonding among nonkinswomen in Tidewater.

We began the inquiry by asking the respondents whether we are unkind to each other. More than half of the women answering this question agreed that such was the case, but the younger women had this opinion more often than women over forty. As mentioned in Chapter 3, we also found a relationship between what goes on at home and the nature of interpersonal relations with other Black women in Tidewater, a view held by a larger percentage of women over forty than under forty.

Next, we turned to the categories of unkind behavior among women in this region. The results indicate that the largest percentage of the respondents noted that criticism, failure to speak and talk with each other, when misunderstandings developed, and failure to cooperate in social club endeavors, unless friends were in charge, were the most frequent types of unkind behavior among us. A smaller percentage of the respondents reported that we engaged in stressful conversation, but almost twice as many women under as over forty held this opinion. These types of unkind behavior among us date back to slavery (Stampp 1963) and was also known in the mid 1930's, early 1940's (Dollard

1937; Davis and the Gardners 1941; Johnson 1941), and sixties (Kardiner and Ovesey 1962). We also found that in Tidewater, unkind behavior among us was centered mainly around jealousy, our children's relations, and our men.

Empirical evidence in Chapter 4 supports this finding and indicates that a majority of unkind behavior among us took place in dyads. Hence, jealousy was most vivid in personal encounters; we became jealous of job titles, promotions, physical appearance, furniture, cars, homes, and men. Moreover it appears that jealousy was strongest among women in low rent housing areas, for they had a "sense of being trapped."

Unkind behavior centered around children's experiences also took place in dyads. It occurred because of disagreements between children, but it would seem that mothers took such disagreements more seriously than their children, a probable consequence of material and emotional deprivation. Besides, perhaps verbal matches between mothers satisfied such needs as status and attention; furthermore, in all probabilty, the interaction among mothers on all social levels inadvertently socialized the children in the same types of behavior; for example, Dollard (1941) found that adolescent cliques modeled their behavior after upper class adults. Similar to jealousy and children's experiences, stress in interpersonal relations about our men also took place in dyads. The findings indicate that we expended a great deal of time and energy attempting to prevent other women from gaining access to our husbands and attempting to gain access to other women's husbands. When there was such problem, we demonstrated unkind behavior, such as harsh voice tones, harsh statements, and telephone arguments. It is concluded that such dyadic relations enhanced the men's self concept, but perhaps lowered our self-image.

Because only Black middle class women were privy to membership in most voluntary associations, the church excepted clique behavior in formal organizations was most evident in this group. Just as Davis and the Gardners (1941) and Kardiner and Ovesey (1962) found that stress characterized relations among women in community groups, cliques in one Tidewater female organization created antagonism between themselves and other members. These findings indicate that, regardless of social class, stress characterized the relations that we experienced with each other in Tidewater.

Our findings also indicate that we responded three ways to the unkind behavior of each other. We returned unkind words and actions, socialized only with women known to be friendly, and withdrew from groups unfriendly to us. It thus appears that our relations with each other had a very limiting effect. Perhaps they hindered our full social development and enjoyment and deprived us of some rewarding experiences with women who shared our burdens of race and sex. But the good news is that, hopefully, this awareness study will encourage us to put down our sword and "study war no more."

REFERENCE CITED

Davis, Allison and Burleigh B. and Mary R. Gardner
    1941   DEEP SOUTH. Chicago: The University of Chicago Press.

CHAPTER SIX

IMPLICATIONS

Introduction

This study has focused on Black women's experiences in Tidewater in the workplace, home, and community. It identified problems that we experience in each of these settings. The problems in the workplace include weak employer-employee interpersonal behavior, job discrimination, job protest, and job injustice while the need for us to work and help support the household, the use some of our husbands make of their paycheck, our husbands' role in the decision making process and household repairs, and emotional relations are major problems in our homes. On the other hand, jealousy, children's problems, men, and cliques in organizations are sources of problems in the community. Black women's problems in Tidewater reflect larger class issues in the society, as well as the regions of our lives. They require personal and group action along with policy to ease our burden in Tidewater.

Problems of Black Women and Larger Class Issues in Tidewater

As shown in Chapter 1, historically, Blacks occupied a caste position in the American society vis à vis whites (Davis and the Gardners 1941; Kardiner and Ovesey 1962; Dollard 1937; Johnson 1941). It also shows that each caste was comprised of female cliques made up of the most prestigious women and the women directly below them, and that these two groups experienced mutual antagonism. Not only was there antagonism at the top, but there was also antagonism between lower class parents and upper class parents (Davis and the Gardners) and mutual antagonism sometimes caused small clubs to disband (Kardiner and Ovesey). These findings indicate that Blacks not only comprised a caste, but there were also vivid lines of demarcation between social classes, in the lower caste, and within classes. What our study of Black women indicates is that, since the first half of this century, our circumstances have changed very little. Because we continue to interact with white men and women on a caste-like basis, because we continue to interact with Black men and Black women on a caste-like basis, our circumstances not only reflect the past, but they also reflect current larger class issues in the society. One such issue is that we comprise the bottom rung of the status system in Tidewater while another larger issue is that we belong to a quadruple caste system. Such multiple burdens of life result in economic, social, and emotional depravity for all of us Black women in Tidewater. The question these findings raise is what are the ways out?

Implications For Individuals, Groups and Policies

This section of the chapter deals with some ways to lessen the quadruple burden of Black women in this region. It appears that a multifaceted approach is needed in the workplace, home, and community. Beginning with the workplace, we believe the initial step has to be taken by each individual Black woman, a conclusion somewhat supported by Hall (1981:167) when he noted that "the greatest amount of solace and support that the Black male can depend upon in order to cope with the stress and the pressures of the times is still internal." Another individual approach to our problems in the workplace is for us to use the proper channels and demeanor and perform our tasks efficiently and seek our deserved wages, promotions, job evaluations, and job benefits. On the other hand, adult women who have not made excellence their motto and who are reluctant to seek their just rewards, should begin practicing now. The implementation of this system is likely to improve our self concept and economic success, lessen our tensions, improve our race, and enhance the economic standing of the society.

The next approach to improving interpersonal relations and job justice in the workplace, in Tidewater, is group action. Such group action should begin with us. This approach is explained by Asante (1981:82) who noted that "The Afrocentric-drive to create must always be based on a deep collective commitment to excellence." Hence, when each of us dedicates ourselves to excellence in the workplace, such collective action is bound to result in some relief from our work-related problems.

Concomitant with our group action, other types of group action, including peer networks, are needed to remedy our job relations. According to Nieva and Gutek (1982:56), "inclusion in informal networks is necessary to career success." Participation in networks in the workplace

131

would do a great deal for us, because they would enable us to learn about job openings, new jobs on the drawing board, people important to success, jobs due to become vacant, and nature of employers, factors that contribute to promotions, jobs, and raises. Still another group approach to improving interpersonal relations and job justice is for us to become a protégé of a mentor, journeyman, supervisor, or their equivalent. The protégé-mentor relationship is a special case of the general social networks, through which individuals get assimilated into the system (Nieva and Gutek 1982:57). A woman, of any age, who enters the workplace, should seek a mentor, without regard for age, race, or sex, who is willing to help develop her skills and give special advice, inside information, critical experiences, and social status by mutual association, as is frequently the case with white male employees (Becker and Strauss 1956:253-263; Epstein 1970:965-982; Wells 1973:20-24).

The problems of Black women in the workplace also have some implications for community groups in Tidewater. They could resocialize adult females, in workshops, to get jobs and perform duties efficiently and pleasantly for all employer types. Moreover, community groups, including the church, could make available training programs, staffed by highly competent personnel, practitioners, and scholars, that provide instruction in occupations and related careers in the labor market.

We believe that individual and group actions would do much to improve our experiences in the workplace, however, they are insufficient. They should be coupled with policy making and implementation by all companies hiring minority women, in particular, and women in general. One such policy should focus on an improved employer type, achieved through effective training. Because Black women may be able to perform tasks more efficiently, if employers show more job appreciation and friendliness, give more job compliments, treat employees with a great deal of respect and demonstrate fairness in job assignments, raises, and promotions, such policies for upgrading employers and their job effectiveness would enhance productivity. A second policy needed in the workplace is an improved complaint system. Each place of work should provide a fair, simplistic, efficient, and clearly defined system for female employees to obtain remedies from unfair labor practices.

Now let us turn to ways of overcoming our problems in the home. Writing about Black men, Braithwaite (1981:95) suggests the need and some ways that would probably improve the quality of relations between Black men and Black women. They require that: "Black men and Black women address unsatisfactory interpersonal relationships by participating in personal growth and human relations group sessions; that universities develop and include a course on male and female relationships as a part of their general education and continuing education curriculum; and that Black national organizations place on their program agenda the issues of strategies for strengthening relationships between Black women and Black men" (Braithwaite 1981:95).

On the basis of this Tidewater study about Black women, we suggest a number of other ways, including family socialization, to extricate us from problems in the home. For example, husband infidelity, husband failure to be warm and loving toward their wives, husband failure to participate in decision making, and husbands' lack of mechanical knowledge to do household repairs could be greatly curtailed through improved childhood socialization. Besides, the family, community, church, and school groups could sponsor childhood socialization workshops for newlyweds and parents with young children to teach them how to assist their children in developing expertise in household matters and the need to teach their children how to feel good about themselves, along with the importance of demonstrating their love to them. Such parental training would equip us to socialize our children in effective behavior. There is another dimension that should be added to workshops that focus on adult male-female behavior. They could teach us to select spouses on our socioeconomic level and spend less time complaining about their shortcomings and more time enhancing their ego and progress. Along the same line, Rutledge (1980:157) states that "every aspect of marital interaction goals is indicative of marital "strengths." In addition, churches, graduate and undergraduate chapters of fraternities and other men's organizations could sponsor ongoing training programs for adult men that focus on major aspects of their lives, including relations with Black women.

The Community

Let us now turn to the final environment, the community, where Black women, in Tidewater, face problems. On the basis of the findings in this study, it appears that groups can do a great deal to lessen mutual female oppression. One way to break the cycle is for the family to drastically improve its childhood socialization process. Young girls and boys should be taught not to joke each other, for it is likely to be one training ground for child-female antagonism that extends into adulthood. Moreover, mothers should teach their young children, by precept and example, not to antagonize other females. Similarly, mothers could teach, by example, how to forgive women, when misunderstandings arise. Another way that mutual female antagonism can be curtailed is by community groups, such as graduate and undergraduate chapters of fraternities and sororities and social clubs and churches, sponsoring educational programs on the prevention of intra-race female abuse. Further, the family, church, and other local groups could include, in their program, procedures for resocializing Blacks to respect blackness. Once appreciation for blackness becomes a reality in the Black conscience, there is likely to be a noticeable decline in Black racism. Once Black female racism has been eliminated, at least one oppresive hurdle will be cleared. It is necessary to seek justice from white men and white women and Black men, but it appears that we would move quickly to eliminate mutual feminine problems that we, ourselves, perpetuate. Though, as my students have often pointed out, there is the opinion, among some of us, that whites initiated divisiveness, in our race, during slavery, it must be kept in mind that, as a group, it is up to us to end it. Because white racism is severe, it should be easy for us to bind together and assure every Black woman in Tidewater, by our actions and words, that we will never abridge her freedom and happiness. This is, indeed, a challenge that is within our reach, that we hope every Black woman in Tidewater will accept.

Because the findings in this study were taken from the lives of Black women in the Tidewater region, they can be used to find solutions to many of our problems. With the identification of such problems, it is clear that the workplace, home, and community need to reinforce the same values, such as love, respect, hard work, efficiency, pride of accomplishment, fairness, and effective leadership. Reinforcement can take many forms, including precept and example and training programs, as suggested earlier, in each environment, conducted by community agencies, churches, and social and civic groups. With solutions to our problems, the quality of life will go up in the workplace, home, community, and the larger Tidewater region.

REFERENCES CITED

Asante, Molefi
1981 "Black Male and Female Relationships." In Lawrence E. Gary (ed.) BLACK MEN. Beverly Hills: Sage Publications, pp. 75-82.

Becker, Howard S. and L. Strauss
1953 "Careers, Personality and Adult Socialization." AMERICAN JOURNAL OF SOCIOLOGY 62:253-263.

Braithwaite, Ronald L.
1981 "Interpersonal Relations Between Black Males and Black Females." In Lawrence E. Gary (ed.) BLACK MEN. Beverly Hills: Sage Publications, pp. 83-95.

Epstein, C.
1970 "Encountering the Male Establishment: Sex Status Limits on Women's Careers in the Professions." AMERICAN JOURNAL OF SOCIOLOGY 75:965-982.

Hall, Leland K.
1981 "Support Systems and Coping Patterns." In Lawrence E. Gary (ed.) BLACK MEN. Beverly Hills: Sage Publications, pp. 159-167.

Nieva, Veronica F. and Barbara A. Gutek
1982 WOMEN AND WORK. New York: Praeger.

Puryear, Gwendolyn Randall
1980 "The Black Women: Liberated or Oppressed." In Beverly Lindsay (ed.) COMPARATIVE PERSPECTIVES OF THIRD WORLD MOVEMENT. New York: Praeger.

Rutledge, Essie Manuel
1980 "Marital Interaction Goals of Black Women: Strengths and Effects." In La Frances Rodgers-Rose (ed.) THE BLACK

WOMAN. Beverly Hills: Sage Publications, pp. 145-159.

Wells, T.
1973   "Equalizing Advancement Between Women and Men." TRAIN-
ING AND DEVELOPMENTAL JOURNAL 27:20-24.

BIBLIOGRAPHY

Addison, Donald P.
1983   "Black Wives: Perspectives About Their Husbands and Them-
        selves." In Constance E. Obudho (ed.) BLACK MARRIAGE
        AND FAMILY THERAPY. Westport: Greenwood Press.

Alexis, Marcus
1974   "The Political Economy of Labor Market Discrimination:
        Synthesis and Exploration." In A. Von Furstenberg (eds.)
        PATTERNS OF DISCRIMINATION, Vol. II. Lexington:
        D.C. Heath Co., pp. 63-83.

Allen, Walter R.
1983   "Race Differences in Husband-Wife Interpersonal Relation-
        ships During the Middle Years of Marriage." In Constance
        E. Obudho (ed.) BLACK MARRIAGE AND FAMILY THER-
        APY. Westport: Greenwood Press.

Asante, Molefi K.
1981   "Black Male and Female Relationships." In Lawrence E.
        Gary (ed.) BLACK MEN. Beverly Hills: Sage Publishers.

Ash, Philip
1972   "Job Satisfaction Differences Among Women of Different
        Ethnic Groups." THE JOURNAL OF VOCATIONAL BEHAV-
        IOR 4:495-507.

Barnes, Annie S.
1971   "The Black Family in Golden Towers." Charlottesville:
        University of Virginia. Dissertation.

Barnes, Annie S.
1975   "The Black Beauty Parlor Complex in A Southern City."
        PHYLON 36:149-154.

Barnes, Annie S.
1977   "The Economic and Social Structure of the Atlanta Commun-
        ity." JOURNAL OF SOCIAL AND BEHAVIORAL SCIENCES
        238:353-360.

Barnes, Annie S.
1979   "Voluntary Association Participation." TENNESSEE AN-
        THROPOLOGIST 4:129-139.

Barnes, Annie S.
1979   "An Urban Voluntary Association." PHYLON XL:264-269.

Barnes, Annie S.
1981   "The Black Kinship System." PHYLON XLII 369-380.

Barnes, Annie S.
1983   "Black Husbands and Wives: An Assessment of marital
        Roles in A Middle Class Neighborhood." In Constance E.
        Obudho (ed.) CONTEMPORARY BLACK MARRAIGES
        AND FAMILY LIFE. Westport: Greenwood Press, pp. 55-73.

Beal, Frances M
1975   "Slave of A Slave No More: Black Women in Struggle."
        THE BLACK SCHOLAR 6:2-10.

Becker, Gary
1957   "THE ECONOMICS OF DISCRIMINATION." Chicago: The
        University of Chicago Press.

Becker, H. S. and Strauss, A. L.
1953   "Careers, Personality and Adult Socialization." AMERICAN
        JOURNAL OF SOCIOLOGY 62:253-263.

Bernard, Jessie
1966   MARRIAGE AND FAMILY AMONG NEGROES. Englewood
        Cliffs: Prentice-Hall.

Billingsley, Andrew T.
1968   BLACK FAMILIES IN WHITE AMERICA. Englewood CLiffs:
        Prentice-Hall.

Blood, Robert O. and Donald M. Wolfe
1960   HUSBANDS AND WIVES. New York: Free Press.

Blubaugh, Jon A. and Dorothy L. Pennington
1976   CROSSING DIFFERENCE. . .INTERRACIAL COMMUNICA-
TION. Columbus, Ohio: Charles E. Merrill Publishing Company.

Boggs, James
1972   "Blacks in the Cities: Agenda for the 70s." THE BLACK
SCHOLAR 4:50-61.

Braithwaite, Ronald L.
1981   "Interpersonal Relations Between Black Males and Black
Females." In Lawrence E. Gary (ed.) BLACK MEN. Beverly
Hills: Sage Publishers.

Brimmer, Andrew
1978   "Economic Perspectives." BLACK ENTERPRISE 9:57

Brimmer, Andrew
1978   "Economic Perspectives." BLACK ENTERPRISE 9:120

Brink, William and Louis Harris
1964   THE NEGRO REVOLUTION. New York: Simon & Schuster.

Brown, Hallie Q.
1971   HOMESPUN HEROINES AND OTHER WOMEN OF DISTINC-
TION. Freeport: Books for Libraries Press.

Bullock, Henry Allen
1941   THE TEXAS NEGRO FAMILY: THE STATUS OF ITS SOCIO-
ECONOMIC ORGANIZATION. Prairie View: Prairie View
College Press.

Carvell, Fred J.
1970   HUMAN RELATIONS IN BUSINESS. New York: The MacMillan Company.

Champagne, Joseph E. and Donald C. King
1967   "Job Satisfaction Factors Among Underprivileged Workers."
THE PERSONNEL AND GUIDANCE JOURNAL 5:429-434.

Chisholm, Shirley
1970   "Racism and Anti-Feminism." THE BLACK SCHOLAR
34:40-45.

Cromwell, Vicky L. and Ronald E. Cromwell
1978   "Perceived Dominance in Decision-Making and Conflict
        Resolution among Anglo, Black and Chicano Couples."
        JOURNAL OF MARRIAGE AND THE FAMILY 40:749-759.

Davis, Allison and Burleigh B. and Mary R. Gardner
1941   DEEP SOUTH. Chicago: The University of Chicago Press.

Dollard, John
1937   CASTE AND CLASS IN A SOUTHERN TOWN. New York:
        Doubleday & CO.

Downs, Karl E.
1943   MEET THE NEGRO. Pasadena: The Login Press.

Drake, St. Clair and Horace R. Cayton
1945   BLACK METROPOLIS, II. New York: Harper and Row
        Publishers

Dubois, W. E. B.
1898   SOME EFFECTS OF AMERICAN NEGROES FOR THEIR
        BETTERMENT. Atlanta: Atlanta University Press.

Epstein, C.
1970   "Encountering the Male Establishment: Sex Status Limits
        on Women's Careers in the Professions." AMERICAN JOUR-
        NAL OF SOCIOLOGY 75:965-982.

Feagin, Joe R. and Douglas Lee Eckberg
19   "Discrimination: Motivation, Action, Effects, and Context."
        ANNUAL REVIEWS OF SOCIOLOGY 6:9.

Feagin, Joe R. and Clairece Booher Feagin
1978   DISCRIMINATION AMERICAN STYLE (Institutional Racism
        and Sexism). Englewood Cliffs: Prentice-Hall, Inc.

Frazier, E. Franklin
1932   THE FREE NEGRO FAMILY. Nashville: Fisk University
        Press.

Frazier, E. Franklin
1939   THE NEGRO FAMILY IN THE UNITED STATES. Chicago:
        The University of Chicago Press.

Frazier, E. Franklin
1957   THE BLACK BOURGEOISIE. New York: Free Press.

Friedlander, Frank and Stuart Greenberg
1971   "Effects of Job Attitudes, Training, and Organization Climate
        on Performance of the Hard Core Unemployed." APPLIED
        PSYCHOLOGY 4:287-295.

Gibson, D. Parke
1978   "Money: How We Earn It and How We Spend It." THE BLACK
        COLLEGIAN 9:20,22.

Ginzberg, Eli and Dale E. Hiestand
1966   "Employment Patterns of Negro Men and Women." In John
        P. Davis (ed.) THE AMERICAN NEGRO REFERENCE BOOK.
        Englewood Cliffs: Prentice-Hall, Inc.

Greenhaus, Jeffery H. and James F. Gavin
1972   "The Relationship Between Expectancies and Job Behavior
        for White and Black Employees." PERSONNEL PSYCHOL-
        OGY 3:449-455.

Gurin, Patricia
1977   "The Role of Worker Expectancies in the Study of Employ-
        ment Discrimination." In Phyllis A. Wallace and Annette
        M. Lamond (eds.) WOMEN, MINORITIES AND EMPLOYMENT
        DISCRIMINATION. Lexington, Mass: D.C. Heath & Co.,
        pp. 13-37.

Gutman, Herbert G.
1976   THE BLACK FAMILY IN SLAVERY AND FREEDOM,
        1750-1925. New York: Pantheon Press.

Hall, Leland K.
1981   "Support Systems and Coping Patterns." In Lawrence E.
        Gary (ed.) BLACK MEN. Beverly Hills: Sage Publishers.

Hawkins, Homer
1976   "Urban Housing and the Black Family." PHYLON 37:73-84.

Hemmons, Willa Mae
1980   "The Women's Liberation Movement: Understanding Black
        Women's Attitudes." In La Frances Rodgers-Rose (ed.)
        THE BLACK WOMAN. Beverly Hills: Sage Publications.

Hill, Herbert
1977   "Postponement of Economic Equality." THE BLACK SCHOL-
        AR 9:18-23.

Hippler, Arthur E.
1974   HUNTER'S POINT. New York: Basic Books, Inc.

Hood, Elizabeth F.
1978   "Black Women, White Women: Separate Paths to Liberation."
        THE BLACK SCHOLAR 9:45-46.

Holloman, Regina E. and Fannie E. Lewis
1978   "The Clan: Case Study of A Black Extended Family in Chica-
        go." In Demitri B. Shimkin et al. (eds.) THE EXTENDED
        BLACK FAMILY IN BLACK SOCIETIES. The Hague: Mouton
        Publishers, pp. 201-238.

Jack, Lenus, Jr.
1978   "Kinship and Residential Propinquity in Black New Orleans:
        The Wesleys." In Demitri B. Shimkin, et al. (eds.) THE
        EXTENDED FAMILY IN BLACK SOCIETIES. The Hague:
        Mouton Publishers, pp. 239-269.

Johnson, Charles
1941   GROWING UP IN THE BLACK BELT. New York: Schocken
        Books.

Kardiner, Abraham and Lionel Ovesey
1962   THE MARK OF OPPRESSION. New York: The World Publish-
        ing Company, Meridian Books.

King, Charles E.
1945   "The Negro Maternal Family: A Product of An Economic
        and A Culture System." SOCIAL FORCES 24:100-104.

King, Ruth E. G. and Jean T. Griffin
1983   "The Loving Relationship" Impetus for Black Marriage."
        In Constance E. Obudho (ed.) BLACK MARRIAGE AND
        FAMILY THERAPY. Westport: Greenwood Press.

Kunkel, Peter and Sara Sue Kennard
1971   SPOUT SPRING. New York: Holt, Rinehart and Winston,
        Inc.

Krueger, Ann
1963   "The Economics of Discrimination." JOURNAL OF POLITI-
       CAL ECONOMY 3:481-486.

Ladner, Joyce
1972   TOMORROW'S TOMORROW. New York: Doubleday &
       Company.

Lefcourt, Herbert M. and Gordon W. Ladwig
1965   "The American Negro: A Problem in Expectancies." JOUR-
       NAL OF PERSONALITY AND SOCIAL PSYCHOLOGY
       2:377-380.

Lefton, Mark
1968   "Race Expectancies and Anomie." SOCIAL FORCES 46:347-
       352.

Lerner, Gerda
1972   BLACK WOMEN IN WHITE AMERICA. New York: Vintage
       Books.

Liebow, Elliot
1967   TALLY'S CORNER. Boston: Little, Brown and CO.

Lorde, Audre
1979   "We Need Only Look At the Close, Highly Complex, and
       Involved Relationships Between African Co-Wives. . ."
       MS. MAGAZINE 7:52,70.

Lowenberg, James and Ruth Bogin
1976   BLACK WOMEN IN NINETEENTH CENTURY AMERICAN
       LIFE. University Park: The Pennsylvania State University
       Press.

MacIver, R. M.
1970   THE SOCIETY. Chicago: The University of Chicago Press.

Maier, Norman R. F.
1965   PSYCHOLOGY IN INDUSTRY. Boston: Houghton Mifflin
       Company.

Malveaux, Jullianne
1973   "Polar Entities Apart." ESSENCE MAGAZINE 4:48-49.

Marshall, Ray
1977   "Black Employment in the South." In Phyllis A. Wallace
        and Annett M. Lamond (eds.) WOMEN, MINORITIES, AND
        EMPLOYMENT DISCRIMINATION. Lexington: D. C. Heath
        and Company, pp. 57-81.

Martin, Elmer P. and Joanne Mitchell Martin
1978   THE BLACK EXTENDED FAMILY. Chicago: The University
        of Chicago Press.

McAdoo, Harriett Pipes
1979   "Black Kinship." PSYCHOLOGY TODAY 12:67, 69, 70,
        79, 110.

Miller, Herman
1964   RICH MAN, POOR MAN. New York: Thomas Y. Crowell.

Moynihan, Daniel P.
1967   "The Roots of the Problem." In Lee Rainwater and William
        L. Yancey (eds.) THE MOYNIHAN REPORT AND THE
        POLITICS OF CONTROVERSEY. Cambridge: The M.I.T.
        Press.

Munford, C. J.
1972   "Social Structure and Black Revolution." cf. Veronica F.
        Nieva and Barbara A. Gutek, WOMEN AND WORK. New
        York: Praeger.

Murphy, Betty
1971   "From Janitor to Manager." OPPORTUNITY 1:30-33.

Nelson, Charmeynne D.
1975   "Myths About Black Women Workers in America." THE
        BLACK SCHOLAR, pp. 11-15.

Nieva, Veronica F. and Barbara A. Gutek
1982   WOMEN AND WORK. New York: Praeger.

Nivens, Beatryce
1978   "Raises and Promotions: How To Get What You Deserve."
        ESSENCE December :14,17,18.

Nunez, Elizabeth
1974   "Why Black Johnny Can't Write College English." THE
        BLACK SCHOLAR 6:16-18.

Obudho, Constance E.
1983   BLACK MARRIAGE AND FAMILY THERAPY. Westport:
        Greenwood Press.

Otterbein, Keith F.
1966   THE ANDROS ISLANDERS. Lawrence: University of Kansas
        Publishers.

Powdermaker, Hortense
1962   COPPERTOWN: CHANGING AFRICA. New York: Harper
        & Row Publishers.

Pressman, Sonia
1970   "Job Discrimination and the Black Woman." CRISES
        3:103-108.

Puryear, Gwendolyn Randall
1980   "The Black Women: Liberated or Oppressed." In Beverly
        Lindsay (ed.) COMPARATIVE PERSPECTIVES OF THIRD
        WORLD MOVEMENT. New York: Praeger Publisher.

Reed, Julia
1970   "Marriages and Fertility in Black Teachers." THE BLACK
        SCHOLAR 1:22-28.

Reid, Inez Smith
1972   "TOGETHER" BLACK WOMEN. New York: Emerson Hall
        Publishers, Inc.

Rodgers-Rose, La Frances
1980   THE BLACK WOMAN. Beverly Hills: Sage Publications.

Rollins, Charlemagne Hill
1964   THEY SHOWED THE WAY. New York: Thomas Y. Crowell
        Company.

Ross, John C.
1971   BLACK SLAVERY. Westport: Greenwood Publishers Co.

Russell, John
1913   THE FREE NEGRO IN VIRGINIA. Baltimore: Johns Hopkins
        Press.

Rutledge, Essie Manuel
1980   "Marital Interaction Goals of Black Women: Strengths and
        Effects." In La Frances Rodgers-Rose (ed.) THE BLACK
        WOMAN. Beverly Hills: Sage Publications.

Rutledge, Essie Manuel
1983   "Husband and Wife Relationships of Black Men and Women."
        In Constance E. Obudho (ed) BLACK MARRIAGE AND
        FAMILY THERAPY. Westport: Greenwood Press.

Scanzoni, John H.
1971   THE BLACK FAMILY IN MODERN SOCIETY. Boston:
        Allyn & Bacon.

Shepard, L. and R. L. Quinn
1974   "The 1972-73 Quality of Employment Survey." Ann Arbor:
        Survey Research Center.

Shimkin, Demitri B. et al.
1978   "The Black Extended Family: A Basic Rural Institution
        and A Mechanism of Urban Adaptation." In Demitri B.
        Shimkin et al. (eds.) THE EXTENDED FAMILY IN BLACK
        SOCIETY. The Hague: Mouton Publishers, pp. 25-147.

Slaby, Andrew E. and Joan R. Sealy
1973   "Black Liberation, Women's Liberation." AMERICAN JOUR-
        NAL OF PSYCHOLOGY 130:196-199.

Slocum, John W. and Robert H. Strawser
1972   "Racial Differences in Job Attitudes." JOURNAL OF
        APPLIED PSYCHOLOGY 1:28-32.

Smith, Raymond T.
1956   THE NEGRO FAMILY IN BRITISH GUIANA. New York:
        Grove Press.

Smith, Stanley Hugh
1953   FREEDOM TO WORK. New York: Vantage Press, Inc.

Stack, Carol B.
1974   ALL OUR KIN. New York: Harper & Row Publishers.

Stampp, Kenneth M.
1963   THE PECULIAR INSTITUTION. New York: Alfred A. Knopf.

Staples, Robert
1973   THE BLACK WOMAN IN AMERICA. Chicago: Nelson Hall Publishers.

Staples, Robert S.
1977   "The Myth of the Black Matriarchy." In Doris Y. Wilkinson and Ronald L. Taylor (eds.) THE BLACK MALE IN AMERICA. Chicago: Nelson Hall Publishers.

Starobin, Robert S.
1970   INDUSTRIAL SLAVERY IN THE OLD SOUTH. New York: Oxford University Press.

Tumin, Melvin
1967   SOCIAL STRATIFICATION. Englewood Cliffs: Prentice-Hall, Inc.

Turner, Castellano B. and Barbara F. Turner
1983   "Black Families, Social Evaluations and Future Marital Relationships." In Constance E. Obudho (ed.) BLACK MAR-RIAGE AND FAMILY THERAPY. Westport: Greenwood Press.

U.S. Department of Labor
1968-69 THE ATLANTA URBAN EMPLOYMENT SURVEY. Atlanta: Southeastern Regional Office, p. 14.

U.S. Department of Labor
1969   THE ATLANTA URBAN EMPLOYMENT SURVEY. July, 1968-June, 1969. Atlanta: Bureau of Labor Statistics, p. 8.

Vontress, Clemmont E.
1971   "The Black Male Personality." THE BLACK SCHOLAR 2:10-16.

Walker, Lynn
1973   "On Employment Discrimination." ESSENCE 4:24.

Weaver, Charles N.
1974   "The Negro-White Differences in Job Satisfaction." BUSI-
        NESS HORIZONS 1:67-72.

Welch, Finis
1967   "Labor-Market Discrimination: An Interpretation of Income
        Differences in the Rural South." THE JOURNAL OF POLIT-
        ICAL ECONOMY 75:225-240.

Welch, Finis
1973   "Educational and Racial Discrimination." In Orley Ashenfelter
        and Albert Rees (eds.) DISCRIMINATION IN LABOR MAR-
        KETS. Princeton: Princeton University Press.

Wells, T.
1973   "Equalizing Advancement Between Women and Men."
        TRAINING AND DEVELOPMENT JOURNAL 27:20-24

Wernimont, Paul F.
1964   "Intrinsic and Extrinsic Factors in Job Satisfaction." JOUR-
        NAL OF APPLIED PSYCHOLOGY 50:41-50.

Wesley, Charles H.
1960   "Background and Achievement for Negro Americans." THE
        CRISIS 67:133-149.

Williams, J. Sherwood et al.
1974   "Blacks and Southern Poverty." JOURNAL OF SOCIAL
        AND BEHAVIORAL SCIENCES 20:62-71.

Willie, Charles V.
1970   THE FAMILY LIFE OF BLACK PEOPLE. Columbus: Charles
        E. Merrill Publishing Company.

Willie, Charles V.
1976   A NEW LOOK AT BLACK FAMILIES. Bayside: General
        Hall, Inc.

1961   "What the Branches are Doing." THE CRISIS 68:112-116.

ABOUT THE AUTHOR

Annie S. Barnes, Professor of Anthropology and Sociology, at Norfolk State University in Norfolk, Virginia, received her Ph.D. degree in anthropology from the University of Virginia, 1971. Dr. Barnes is one of the few scholars who has done extensive ethnographic research on the Black middle class family. Her major publications include "Negro Residential Patterns in Atlanta, Georgia, 1860-1983, and Their Impact on Public School Mixing" (1983), "Black Husbands and Wives: An Assessment of Marital Roles in A Middle Class Neighborhood" (1983), "Twelve to Eighteen Years Old" (1983), The Black Kinship System" (1981), "The Osudoku: Kinship, Political, and Ceremonial Systems" (1980), and "An Urban Black Voluntary Association" (1979). She has also presented seventeen scientific papers at professional meetings.

In 1985, Dr. Barnes had two major books published by Wyndham Hall Press. The first, **THE BLACK MIDDLE CLASS FAMILY: A Study of Black Subsociety, Neighborhood, and Home in Interaction,** is a landmark data-base study unrivaled in the field since since E. Franklin Frazier's classic study of 1939. The second, **SOCIAL SCIENCE RESEARCH: A SKILLS HANDBOOK,** is a comprehensive introduction for students in the use of clearly defined and practically exemplified research methods in the social sciences, covering the whole range of methods from library information retrieval and utilization skills to data-gathering and the step-by-step procedures in the writing of a solid research paper. This latter book has been endorsed by the Library Research Council.